Great
Natural Breads
Made Easy

Great Natural Breads Made Easy

Simple Ways to Make Healthful Bread

Bernice Hunt

Illustrated by Lauren Jarrett

SQUAREONE
PUBLISHERS

COVER DESIGNER: Jeannie Tudor
EDITOR: Marie Caratozzolo
TYPESETTER: Gary A. Rosenberg and Theresa Wiscovitch
INTERIOR INSTRUCTIONAL ART: Lauren Jarrett

Square One Publishers
115 Herricks Road
Garden City Park, NY 11040
(516) 535-2010 • (877) 900-BOOK
www.SquareOnePublishers.com

Library of Congress Cataloging-in-Publication Data

Hunt, Bernice Kohn.
    Great natural breads made easy : simple ways to make healthful bread /
by Bernice Hunt.
      p. cm.
   Includes index.
   ISBN-13: 978-0-7570-0294-6 (pbk.)
   ISBN-10: 0-7570-0294-3 (pbk.)
   1. Bread. 2. Cookery (Bread) I. Title.

TX769.H84   2007
641.8'15—dc22

                                           2006029428

Printed in Canada

10   9   8   7   6   5   4   3   2   1

Contents

For Morton,
my partner and best friend,
with my love

Acknowledgments

I am grateful to my husband, Morton, for his enthusiastic and able assistance as my sous-chef, and for his amazing willingness to consume all the bread I can bake.

Very special thanks, too, to Emmy Hartley, my ever-trustworthy taster and critic.

Introduction

The title of this book promises that it will make bread baking easy. Let me explain.

"Easy" means that with very few exceptions, the recipes can be completed in minimal time. None requires highly specialized equipment or exceptional talent. While a few basic utensils are necessary, they are all items you probably have in your kitchen anyway; there are no machines required. This is plain and simple bread making the way your forebears did it long before you were born, and the directions are clear and direct so that you can follow them even if you're a novice.

Although the recipes are simple, the breads are not. The best bakeries feature "artisan" bread—that's the kind I make, and you can make, too. An artisan by definition is "a skilled manual worker," so artisan breads are those that are skillfully made by hand. The skill comes with surprisingly little experience, and once you have learned a few basics and embellished them with your own creativity, you will be able to make magnificent breads that are a joy to create, to behold, and especially, to eat.

Baking bread is a craft, a means of unlimited personal expression even though every baker follows certain age-old steps. It's a particularly rewarding craft because in addition to the pleasure of making the bread itself, when you are done, you will have the even greater pleasure of feeding it to the people you love.

And the people you love will love your bread, and will love taking part in the baking, too. Invite your friends, your spouse, your children into the kitchen. Give any kid, of any age, a lump of dough to knead and form into a loaf of bread, and you will all have a grand time. Guaranteed!

So get ready to bake bread—after brushing up on a bit of history in the opening chapter. All you really need to begin is some flour, and water, and yeast. As soon as you mix them together, you will be creating a kind of magic by connecting to the continuous chain of civilization and culture that began in the mists of the past, long, long before any history had ever been recorded.

PART ONE

THE BASICS

1. The History of Bread

There was no written language when the first bread was baked, but if there had been, the original recipe might have read something like this:

Crush some seeds between two rocks.
Mix the seeds with enough water to make a dough.
Pat the dough into a flat cake.
Put the cake on a flat rock in the sun to bake.

Of course, we can't be sure.

The first bread we *can* be sure about was only a little more sophisticated than the sun-baked flatbread in the fictional recipe above, and it was made by the Neolithic lake dwellers about 8,000 years ago. These ancient people lived in lakeshore houses that were built on stilts in what is now Switzerland. The local waters were rich in minerals, and when some of the settlements were flooded, chemicals in the water petrified many of the objects that were in use at the time. As a result, we know in extraordinary detail how these people lived, and one of the things we know about them is that they baked bread.

When modern archaeologists discovered one of these villages, they found rock-hard loaves of flatbread sitting exactly where they had been left (to cool, perhaps?) by a Stone Age baker. From the evidence, it appears that the lake dwellers cleared fields and planted millet, barley, oats, rye, and wheat. They probably ground the cereal grains between stones and mixed the resulting coarse flour with water to form a dough. After they had shaped the dough into flat loaves, they placed it on rocks and covered it with hot ashes to bake.

From that modest beginning, bread has become a staple food throughout much of the world. It is so important that many people use the word "bread" to signify all food. Who hasn't heard such expressions as "the family breadwinner," "earn your bread," and "break bread with friends"? Even the Lord's Prayer says, "Give us this day our daily bread."

There are many references to bread in the Bible, and the next chapter in the broken history of bread comes from this source. We learn in Genesis that "Lot made a feast and did bake unleavened bread," and in Exodus, we read that the Jews fled Egypt in such a hurry that they had no time to let their bread rise.

Jewish people all over the world commemorate that event by eating unleavened bread called *matzoh* during Passover.

Because there are so many references to unleavened bread in the Old Testament, it is perfectly clear that the people of that time knew how to make leavened (risen) bread. They raised their dough with fermented grain, or sourdough starter, a fascinating procedure still in use today. Bread was certainly important during Biblical times, as most houses had ovens in their yards. We can imagine the women sitting beside these ovens in the sun, grinding the grain with stones.

Bread baking was basic to life throughout the Fertile Crescent (the valleys of the Tigris and Euphrates Rivers in what is now known as Iraq) and further to the East, in the Indus River Valley. As early as 4000 BC, the people of these areas ate a pancake-shaped bread made of barley, sesame seeds, and onions. A similar bread is still made by Iraqi peasants; and flatbreads of various sorts are common throughout the region.

Simple flatbread was the only kind known for many years, but at some point before 3000 BC, the Egyptians dramatically changed bread baking from a standard, mundane procedure into a fine art. We have some knowledge of Egyptian bread because many of the Pharaohs' tombs in the Valley of the Kings have elaborate drawings that show bread being offered to the gods. Forty different kinds of loaves can be found in these pictures. They are round, flat, long and thin, conical, spiral, triangular—and combinations and variations of all these shapes besides.

The Metropolitan Museum of Art in New York City actually has an Eighteenth Dynasty loaf from Thebes that was buried more than 3,400 years ago along with the Princess Meryet-Amum. The bread is disk-shaped and has a hole through its middle. Some of the pictured Egyptian breads look very much like the breads we make today, although the method of manufacture was distinctly different—it is believed that the Egyptians kneaded dough with their feet.

At first, the Egyptians milled barley and wheat with heavy grindstones and mixed the flour with water. Then they shaped the dough into the usual flat cakes and baked them in ovens that had been dug into the ground and lined with clay. As an interesting alternative (invented, perhaps, by someone who had no oven) they also wrapped flat strips of dough around the outsides of earthen jugs and then built fires inside the jugs. Whatever the method of baking, the finished bread was always dense, heavy, and flat because it was unleavened.

But then the Egyptians made an important discovery. Although the Hebrews had long made their bread rise with fermented grain, it was the Egyptians who discovered that it wasn't the sour grain itself that made dough light, but rather the wild yeast plants that flourished in it. Some scholars say that the Egyptians learned to raise pure yeast from spores; others believe that they simply learned they could leaven a new batch of dough with a piece saved from the last baking. Whichever method they used, the Egyptians revolutionized the art of baking bread. Not only did the breads rise uniformly and predictably, but the bakers of Egypt also developed new strains of wheat that could be ground into very fine flour, and they turned out truly fantastic loaves. So inspired were they by their light and airy dough that they began to blend grains together to make a variety of exciting and delicious new textures and flavors. In bursts of unprecedented culinary creativity, they even baked breads that contained such exotic ingredients as honey, almonds, dates, figs, herbs, saffron, and cinnamon. Breads sweetened with honey and fruits and perfumed with spice! No one had ever dreamed of such food. These delicacies, though, were only for the rich; the poor got along, as they had before, with primitive flat cakes made of coarsely ground papyrus reeds (bulrush) and lotus root.

The history of bread takes us next, in a big leap, to ancient Greece during the Classical Period, where a form of barley bread was made. It did not figure importantly in the diet, however, since the Greeks more often made grains into pastes and porridges than into baked goods.

In ancient Rome, though, bread was once more in the forefront. It became so important that in a famous satire, Juvenal wrote that the Romans needed only two things—*panem et circenses,* bread and circuses (entertainment). There were at least sixty-two different kinds of Roman bread, both raised and flat. Bread was distributed free of charge to the needy as an early form of public welfare, and politicians gave it away when they campaigned.

During their first forays into North Africa, the Romans had built a number of aqueducts, which irrigated two thousand miles of coastland; later, that land became extremely fertile and yielded enormous quantities of grain. Egypt had long been a great grain producer, and together, these two sectors of Africa formed a bountiful breadbasket for the Roman Empire.

When the grain arrived in Rome, it was the miller who had to pound and clean it before he could even begin to grind. By the second century AD, the miller had taken over the entire operation and become the baker, too. It may have been at this time that leavened bread was first made in Italy.

Public bakeries had become big business by the time of the early Roman Empire, but even in those days, businesses were subject to occasional setbacks. For example, during the first century AD, all mills had to close when Emperor Caligula decided that his armies needed more draft animals. To fill this need, he "conscripted" all the beasts that were being used to turn the huge grindstones of the mills. Later, in the sixth century, the Goths invaded Rome and cut off the water that was used to turn the water wheels needed by mills.

But in spite of such setbacks, people still managed to bake bread. Accustomed to the occasional "power failures" at the public bakeries, most Romans kept rotary or saddle querns (hand-operated mills) in their homes, so they could grind their own grain just as their ancestors had. The ruins of Pompeii revealed grain mills and ovens in many homes.

Homemade bread was probably cheaper than "store-bought," and people, especially those who were very particular, possibly felt that they could make a better loaf than they could purchase. We know that there was interest in and concern about bread quality, for Galen, the great Greek physician and medical writer who lived from about 130 to 200 AD, told his readers:

> Bread baked in the ashes is heavy and hard to digest because the baking is uneven. That which comes from a small oven or stove causes dyspepsia and is hard to digest. But bread made over a brazier or in a pan, owing to the admixture of oil, is easier to excrete, though steam from the drying makes it rather unwholesome. Bread baked in large ovens, however, excels in all good qualities, for it is well flavored, good for the stomach, easily digested, and very readily assimilated.

Although many of us may think of butter when we think of bread, butter was almost unknown in Greece or Rome. Olive oil was the common household fat, but even that was not used on bread. According to food historian Reay Tannahill in her book *Food in History,* both leavened and plain flatbreads were probably eaten with meat or soaked in wine or milk; the flavored breads were considered meals in themselves and generally were eaten with only a beverage.

Fine breads were enjoyed throughout the Roman Empire. After the Empire's collapse, bread remained to become a staple of the European diet during the Middle Ages. Peasant families commonly ate meals of bread and ale with a bit of salt pork or an onion as accompaniment. The bread was brown, made chiefly of rye, perhaps with some pea and barley flours added. In higher-class households, the bread was made from a mixture of rye and wheat.

From time to time, grain crops were ruined by parasites, causing monstrous famines that swept the continent. There were other calamities, too. One occurred in 857 AD, when a curious and devastating illness struck the population of the Rhine Valley. Perfectly healthy people suddenly began to experience excruciating stomach pains; a short time later, they broke out in fiery rashes, became delirious, and died. The dreaded ailment had come from bread made with rye flour contaminated with a fungus called *ergot*. The affected grain contained twenty known poisons—among them lysergic acid diethymide, better known as LSD. Europeans suffered from repeated outbreaks of ergotism. They called the disease "holy fire" because those who were afflicted were driven mad by the unbearable skin rash.

During the next hundred years, Europe experienced twenty major famines—some lasting for several years. But in spite of such enormous setbacks, the art of agriculture continued to advance, and as it did, bread grew ever more popular. It even became more than just a food. In medieval Europe, only the extremely wealthy had plates and drinking cups. No one, however, had forks; the rich and poor alike ate with their fingers. The usual method of dining was to reach into a common bowl, lift out a piece of food, and drop it onto a *trencher*, a thick square of unleavened bread that was generally shared by two diners. This absorbent "plate" soaked up juices and gravy. When the meal was over, the very poor ate their trenchers, but those who were better off gave them to beggars or threw them to the dogs.

In Britain, as on the Continent, bread grew in importance during the Middle Ages and became unquestionably established as the staple food of the land. In fact, by 1155, London bakers had formed a bakers' brotherhood, a sort of union. In Continental Europe, however, bakers' guilds were not for the benefit of bakers, but rather for protecting the public. They were the means by which governments controlled and regulated baking. The rules were strict and the punishment for breaking them severe. In Austria, any baker who disobeyed the laws governing the weight of each loaf, its cleanliness, and so forth, was fined, imprisoned, or flogged.

Strict measures weren't confined to Europe or even to such early times. In Turkey during the eighteenth century, several bakers were hanged because their prices were too high. In Turkey and Egypt, bakers who sold lightweight or dirty bread were nailed by an ear to their doorposts.

In Britain, a militant bread consumer with literary aspirations published a pamphlet in 1757. It sold for one shilling sixpence, and its title page announced in a large scare headline: **POISON DETECTED.** With totally mystifying punctuation, the page continued:

or
Frightful Truths;
and
Alarming to the British Metropolis.
IN A TREATISE ON BREAD
and the
Abuses practiced in making that Food,
As occasioning the decrease and degeneracy
of the people; destroying infants;
and producing innumerable diseases.
Shewing also,
The virtues of GOOD BREAD, *and*
the manner of making it.
To which is added,
a CHARGE *to the confederacy of bakers,*
corn-dealers, farmers, and millers;
concerning short weight, adulterations,
and artificial scarcities; with easy
methods to prevent all such abuses.
BY MY FRIEND, *a Physician.*

By the time the good physician wrote his treatise, bread had long been established in the New World. It had come initially with the Spanish explorers, but Cortez had brought wheat to plant, as well as the finished product, and one of his servants sowed the seeds in Mexico. It did well, and the first crop was harvested in 1530.

When the early New England colonists arrived, they, too, planted wheat they had brought from Europe. While they waited for it to mature, they learned from the Indians how to grind corn and make cornmeal bread.

The first wheat crops were ready in 1621, and as the colonies grew, each one built a community baking oven. In order to make bread, families had to grind their own wheat, a time-consuming and laborious process. But in 1626, Peter Minuit, first governor of New Amsterdam, had a public mill built on Manhattan Island. Immediately, New York became the milling center of the colonies and remained so until 1750, when Philadelphia took over. By that time, the gristmill, powered by water or wind, had become a familiar sight in all the colonies; but in 1736, there had been a monumental development: a flour mill powered by the exciting new steam engine, which ushered in a new era.

Though steam as a power source was revolutionary, all mills still ground with millstones. Larger and somewhat more sophisticated versions of the earlier grinding tools, millstones were simply two flat stones that rubbed grain between their surfaces. They remained in use until the middle of the nineteenth century. It was at that time that a sensational new flour-making process that used rollers instead of grindstones was developed in Hungary.

Hungarian flour suddenly became the finest, lightest, and whitest the world had ever seen. Word of this success was of special interest in what was then the northwestern sector of the United States. Although this area produced an abundant amount of wheat, it was harder than the variety that grew in warmer climates. Furthermore, a large part of the wheat was wasted when it was ground in the gristmills. After learning of the new Hungarian process, the governor of Minnesota felt that it might be just what was needed to transform the problem wheat into an outstanding cash crop. He sent for a team of Hungarian engineers who set up a roller mill in Minneapolis. It was an instant success.

The hard wheat passed through a series of rollers that grew successively smaller in size, making it possible for the flour to be milled with a minimum of waste. Then the flour passed through sieves of increasing fineness, a process known as *bolting.* Bolted flour is light and airy, and when baked, it rises higher than coarser flour. Everyone wanted the new flour, and Minneapolis soon became a great milling center.

As the milling industry grew, so did commercial bakeries. Virtually unknown until this time, "store" bread gained such popularity that by the start of World War I, it was obvious that home bread baking was becoming a thing of the past. Since that time, commercial baking has been one of the giant industries of our nation. Entire generations of Americans never knew of any bread but the fluffy white spongy loaf that comes sliced and wrapped from gleaming machines. Convenient? Yes. But the products are typically filled with additives and preservatives, and devoid of any real nutritional goodness. This "sanitary" bread marked a true low point in the annals of bread history.

Fortunately, around 1960, a new and quickly burgeoning interest in foods that were natural, wholesome, and homemade developed in the United States. Although there had always been a stubborn handful of home bakers, suddenly there was a great surge of bread baking in communes and among the back-to-the-land people. The trend caught on and began to spread throughout the nation. Within ten years, homemade bread had stopped being a rarity and, in fact, was becoming commonplace again. And it was not only housewives who were baking bread this time; it was men, working women, sons, and daughters. Americans knew a good thing when they tasted it. They also enjoyed *making* it.

Homemade bread does take some time and effort, so it may never totally displace the many millions of commercial loaves that are still sold daily. But as more and more people experience the joy of baking, the word continues to spread. Today, the kitchens of America are producing more loaves of bread than they have in more than fifty years, and the number increases every day.

2. A Loaf of Bread . . . The Basics

A Jug of Wine, a Loaf of Bread—and Thou
Beside me singing in the Wilderness—

So wrote the Persian poet Omar Khayyam, describing a personal vision of paradise. Surely the bread Omar had in mind was soft and tender with a crunchy crust (perhaps still warm from the oven) and enveloped in a heavenly fragrance. Since the poet died in 1123 we can't be sure of the details, but one thing we can be absolutely certain of is that the immortalized bread he spoke of did not come from a supermarket.

It's easy to wax poetic about bread; no other food has been mentioned as often in literature. Bread is unique, too, in its importance in religious ceremonies from earliest times. The Christian sacrament of bread and wine put an "official" stamp on the holy significance bread had in many religious rites that predated Christianity. Perhaps bread was included in those early ceremonies because of its unmistakable aura of magic and mystery—the special quality that comes from the fact that bread dough (or at least the yeast it contains) is alive. Like all living things, yeast dough is never completely predictable, and therein lies the enchantment—and for the baker, the challenge as

well. No matter how carefully you follow the instructions, you can never make the *exact* same bread twice.

Though we know that a baked mixture of flour and water is technically considered "bread," a *loaf* of bread is one that contains yeast or some other leavening agent. So-called "quick breads," which are raised with baking powder, baking soda, or both, are delicious and easy to make, but they are not surrounded by any special mystique. Baking a quick bread is like baking a cake—pleasurable, worthwhile, predictable, routine. But ah, a yeast bread! Baking yeast bread is a life experience that no one should miss.

Before rolling up your sleeves and trying your hand at making your own bread—both yeast loaves and quick breads—it will be helpful to become familiar with some important bread-making basics. After all, you will want to find success with every loaf you make. So consider this chapter a primer of sorts, a place you can turn to for guidance on key ingredients, necessary equipment, and helpful techniques for producing perfect loaves every time.

INGREDIENTS

Starting with the right ingredients is key in baking bread. Flour, water, and yeast head the list of basic bread components, but other ingredients, such as sweeteners and oils, also play significant roles in lending desirable qualities to bread.

YEAST

A yeast bread's magical ingredient—yeast—is actually a microscopic plant. Dormant in its dry state, yeast comes to life as soon as you moisten and feed it. It thrives on water and sugar, but only when the temperature is right. If the liquid is too cold, the yeast will remain inactive; if it is too hot, the yeast will die. Perhaps the need to care for yeast tenderly, to watch over it thoughtfully, to maintain the delicate balance of conditions necessary to keep it alive, creates our mystical relationship with it.

Yeast is not just another food, nor is it just another plant. It is a particular kind of plant cell that buds as it grows. As soon as a bud matures, it breaks off and immediately becomes a new cell, ready to put forth its own bud (or buds). The time it takes yeast to grow a new generation is only about thirty minutes.

When yeast is provided with liquid and carbohydrates, it feeds on the latter, digests it, and begins to bud. And in doing so, it gives off alcohol and carbon dioxide gas. The carbon dioxide bubbles through the dough and puffs it full of tiny holes. It is these gas-filled pockets that make the dough rise until it has the texture of a sponge. When the bread is baked, the oven's heat kills the yeast and eliminates the alcohol. (Wine is made with yeast, too, but the end result is quite different. Grapes supply the sugar and liquid, but as the carbon dioxide forms, it easily passes through the liquid and dissipates in the air. What remains is the alcohol, which, in the case of wine, is the desired end product.)

Though yeast used in bread can get all the food it needs from flour alone, it grows more quickly if it gets a head start from some form of concentrated sugar. That is why many bread recipes contain a small amount of sugar or honey, even if it is not enough to impart any noticeable sweetness to the bread.

Yeast is the most exciting ingredient in bread because it is alive. And like most things that are alive and exciting, it is also rather temperamental, but not nearly as temperamental as it used to be. When yeast first became commercially available, it was sold only in paste form, either in bulk or as a "cake." It had to be kept under refrigeration, and if it wasn't used promptly, the yeast—slowed down by the cold, but still needing some nourishment—soon died. That is why most bread recipes (but not the ones in this book) tell you to *prove* or *proof* the yeast before doing anything else. This term, which is used quite literally, describes a step that "proves" the yeast is alive. The yeast bread recipes in this book call for active dry yeast, a dry, granular yeast that is dormant. There is an expiration date on the package, which you must observe, but as long as the package is unopened and the contents remain dry, the yeast has a very long life and does not need to be refrigerated. (I keep mine in the refrigerator anyway. And if I'm not going to be using it for some time, I put it in the freezer where it will keep almost indefinitely.)

Active dry yeast is commonly available in small quarter-ounce foil packets, which contain one level tablespoon of the product. It also comes in larger packets and in jars. If you are going to be baking bread regularly (and once you begin, you are likely to), it's handier and less expensive to buy the larger size. Just be sure to refrigerate the yeast after the package has been opened, and keep it dry by resealing the package or tightly capping the jar.

As mentioned earlier, dry yeast becomes activated when mixed with liquid, which must be lukewarm — between 110° and 115°F. Remember, if the temperature is too cool, the yeast will grow too slowly; if it's too high, the yeast will die — so be careful. If you have a candy thermometer, use it to determine the correct temperature of the water, and then test it with your finger so you'll know what it is supposed to feel like for future bread-making sessions. If you don't have a suitable thermometer, use water that feels just about right for a new baby's bath — slightly warmer than your fingers, not hot, just comfortably warm.

FLOUR

As soon as the yeast begins to get lively, it needs food, and though you may give it some sugar for a quick start, it will grow mainly on — and in — flour. There are many kinds of flour, and despite the fact that white flour makes the lightest cakes and melt-in-your-mouth pastries, it also makes the least interesting and the least nutritious bread. Whole wheat flour, as its name implies, is made from the entire wheat berry, and is the natural, complete basic bread flour. It has a wonderful wheaty taste and is considered the true "staff of life" because it is so rich in protein, vitamins, and minerals.

A single wheat berry, or grain of wheat, is made up of three parts. The *germ* is the seed, which can grow into a new plant; it is our richest natural source of vitamin B. The fibrous outer hull of the berry is the *bran,* which provides roughage. Researchers have discovered that bran's inclusion in the diet may protect us against a number of serious diseases, including colon cancer. The largest (and least nutritional) part of the wheat berry is the *endosperm,* which is mainly starch and little else. White flour is made from this part of the wheat berry.

The minimal nutritional value of white flour is reduced even further when it is chemically bleached to make it whiter; it is this type of flour that is typically used to make the bland, fluffy, plastic-wrapped bread found on supermarket shelves. Even though the law requires that such bread be "enriched" through the addition of a few vitamins, it doesn't begin to make up for the nutrients that were removed in the first place. The good news is that with the nation's growing awareness of dietary nutrition, commercial bakeries are providing many new wholesome bread varieties. Some are pretty good, too — but still not as good as the ones you make at home.

Believe it or not, you can make a dark, dense, and delicious loaf of hearty homemade bread with the whole wheat flour sold in most supermarkets. If you want the best, look for whole wheat flour that is *stone-ground,* which means it has been milled through the old-fashioned grinding method. This is slower and less efficient than the roller method used in modern milling, but it does not subject the grain to high temperatures as rollers do. As a result, stone-ground whole wheat flour retains its nutritional value; it also has a slightly better taste and more wholesome texture than other types. If, however, stone-ground is unavailable, choose any other whole wheat flour variety.

Although whole wheat flour is nutritionally superior to white, it seems important to note something obvious about white flour — it is necessary for making white bread. Many white breads are wonderful and absolutely delicious, from a simple white loaf, which serves as the basis for dozens of delectable bread varieties, to a more sophisticated creation like the French-style baguette.

You will also need white flour to make many breads that call for a mixture of both white and dark flours. The reason white flour is often mixed with other flours is that it is very rich in *gluten,* a protein that makes dough stretchy and elastic. Some flour varieties, such as rye and soy, have so little gluten that the dough they form does not rise well. In order to use these flours successfully, you have to boost the gluten by adding some wheat flour—usually white—to the dough.

As dough is kneaded, the gluten becomes more and more stretchy. It finally becomes so elastic that when the yeast starts sending out its gas bubbles, the dough begins to puff up, and the many small bubbles that hold the gas remain. Dough that is well kneaded has the consistency of bubble gum. Without gluten—or without yeast—bread would turn out flat, like matzoh or crackers.

So, as you can see, white flour is an important ingredient in many bread recipes. When shopping for it, choose all-purpose unbleached varieties over bleached. Bleached flour has added chemicals to make it whiter. And although unbleached white flour does not contain the nutritional bran and germ found in whole wheat flour, it has better flavor and is better for you than bleached.

All flour should be kept in airtight containers to prevent insect infestation. Specialty flours, such as soy, rye, and semolina, which are usually purchased in small quantities, are best kept in the refrigerator.

FAT

Fat, usually in the form of oil, is sometimes added to bread to make it richer and softer. It also helps the bread stay fresher longer. I prefer oil over butter because it's easier to use (you don't have to melt it), and, unlike butter, it has no cholesterol. You can, however, substitute melted butter for the oil in most of the recipes in this book. Some recipes, such as Rosemary-Olive Oil Bread (page 46) and Olive Bread (page 69), call specifically for olive oil. In such cases, olive oil (preferably extra-virgin) is what you should use.

For sweet breads, you have no choice; for these, you *must* use butter because sweet breads depend on it for their special flavor. When using butter in any recipe, I recommend the unsalted variety, which should always be as fresh as possible. If you don't use

up the butter quickly, wrap it securely and store in a plastic bag in the freezer.

I believe the best all-purpose oils are canola, soy, and corn, but you can use any light vegetable cooking oil, as long as it doesn't contain saturated or trans fats. And if you love the flavor of olive oil (as I do), feel free to use it in any bread recipe, even though it isn't specified.

SWEETENERS

Honey is called for in many of the recipes in this book, but you can substitute an equivalent amount of white sugar, brown sugar, or molasses if you want to (even though they have different flavors). These sweeteners also have somewhat different potencies, but for bread recipes in which only small quantities are used, it doesn't really matter. Do, however, keep in mind that molasses, which has a very distinctive flavor, is used in some of the dark breads. Be aware that substituting sugar for molasses will make the bread taste quite different (and will lighten the color); so unless you particularly dislike molasses, do not make this change.

Finally, if you use a liquid sweetener like honey or molasses instead of sugar, you might have to use a little extra flour, but this shouldn't make a difference. Remember, the amount of flour in yeast breads is variable anyway.

MILK

Some bread contains milk, which gives it a fine texture, as well as added nutrients. For the sake of convenience, all of the yeast recipes in this book call for powdered dry skim milk. Regular milk needs to be scalded first and then cooled to lukewarm (to avoid killing the yeast). Dry milk, which has already been scalded during its preparation, allows you to skip this step. Simply mix it with water.

EGGS

Adding egg to a yeast bread recipe results in a loaf with added richness and a "cakey" texture. Eggs also participate in the rising action of quick breads and muffins. I do not recommend using egg substitute.

BAKING SODA AND BAKING POWDER

Baking powder and baking soda are the most commonly used leavening agents for quick breads. Before using, be sure to check the expiration date on the package.

SALT AND OTHER FLAVOR ENHANCERS

Salt enhances the flavor of all breads. I use only kosher salt or sea salt for cooking and baking because they are free of added chemicals and have good fla-vor. Both are fairly coarse, although sea salt comes in many grinds. When my recipes call simply for "salt," I am referring to kosher salt. For recipes, such as Focaccia bread and soft pretzels, that call for "coarse salt" to use as a topping, use coarse sea salt. (Do not, however, use the *very* coarse lumps that are used in salt grinders.) Ordinary table salt is ground finer that the others; if this is the type you use, you might want to use just a little less than what the recipe calls for.

Along with salt and sweeteners, today's breads may contain such ingredients as assorted spices, herbs, fruits, fruit juices, saffron, vegetables, nuts, seeds, meals, and whole grains to enhance the flavor and/or to add texture.

WATER

Water is often a matter of preference. I have always found ordinary tap water to be acceptable; however, if yours has a distinctive taste, you might want to use bottled water instead.

EQUIPMENT

One of the beauties of bread baking—aside from its delicious results—is that it requires just a few common utensils and pieces of equipment, which you may already own. Some baking pans and mixing bowls, measuring cups and spoons, and few other basic items are all that you'll need.

MEASURING CUPS AND SPOONS

Although you can get along with a one-cup-size measuring cup, it's handy to have a two-cup, or a four-cup size as well. You'll also need a teaspoon and tablespoon for measuring small amounts of various ingredients, such as baking powder, salt, herbs, and spices. Measuring spoons generally come in a basic set of four and include measurements for one-quarter, one-half, and one full teaspoon, as well as one table-spoon. If you already have them, use them, otherwise use your everyday spoons and judge the fractions.

BREAD PANS AND BAKING SHEETS

Since homemade yeast bread seems to get eaten very fast, I find that it doesn't pay to make just a single loaf. Almost all the recipes that follow make two loaves; therefore, if you are going to bake your bread in loaf pans, you will need at least two. A standard or large-sized bread pan is roughly 9 x 5 inches; a medi-um-sized pan is about 8 x 4 inches. Smaller pans are available in a variety of sizes, as are U-shaped French baguette pans, which are generally attached in pairs like Siamese twins. I hand-shape most of my breads and bake them on an 18-x-13-inch flat baking sheet (an uninsulated cookie sheet or what is known technically as a half-sheet pan). When it comes to all bread pans and baking sheets, please note that the sizes just mentioned may vary somewhat with different manufacturers; but this size variation is insignificant. It is not necessary or even practical to be absolutely precise about pan size because yeast bread doughs vary widely in volume. Rely on your eye—and common sense.

If you don't have bread pans and are planning to buy some, there are many kinds from which to choose. The very best are made of extremely heavy black steel (called baker's steel). They hold the heat well and develop loaves with a marvelous crust. They are, however, quite expensive. More moderate in price, yet completely satisfactory in every way, are nonstick pans. I do, however, recommend greasing these pans in spite of their nonstick coating. This way, you will never have to worry about getting your bread out of the pan in one piece. Finally, if you happen to already have plain loaf pans made of glass, aluminum, or another metal, they will do perfectly well, too. *When using glass pans, you must remember to lower the oven temperature called for in the recipe by 25°F.*

If you don't want to bother with pans, bake your bread in any ovenproof container that isn't smaller at the top than it is at the bottom. Soufflé and casserole

The Artisan Baker

Part of the fun of baking bread is using your creativity to shape the loaves. Although certain breads are traditionally made in the same shape—Challah (page 44) is formed into a braided or round loaf, while English Cottage Bread (page 34) is always round with a knob on top—many other breads can be twisted and turned into a variety of shapes and sizes. Each recipe in this book includes a *yield* that tells you the number of loaves of a particular size and shape you can make. But don't feel bound to do exactly that. For example, the recipe for Roadside Potato Bread (page 41) yields 2 large loaves that are baked in 9-x-5-inch bread pans; but you can choose to form the dough into 2 large rounds and bake them on a baking sheet instead.

If you decide to vary from the suggested loaf shapes for the yeast breads in this book, let the following chart serve as your guide:

Dough made with 6 to 8 cups of flour can generally yield any of the following:
- 2 large loaves, rounds, or baguettes
- 3 medium loaves, rounds, or baguettes
- a larger number of smaller shaped loaves or rolls

Baking time will vary only a little for large- and medium-size breads, but if you are making rolls or other very small breads, judge the baking time by the color; most rolls take no more than 30 minutes.

dishes, small roasters, even clay flowerpots are all usable. Size doesn't matter as long as you don't fill any container much more than halfway. To bake in a clay flowerpot, make sure it's clean (good bread may be earthy, but you don't want it to taste like earth). Place a circle of foil in the bottom of the pot to cover the hole, and when you grease the pot, grease the foil, too.

Metal coffee cans, both one- and two-pound sizes, also make very attractive breads. Keep in mind that because of a coffee can's deep cylindrical shape and ridges, it can be hard to remove the baked bread. For this reason, it is important to grease the can especially well. For loaves made with yeast, you can also sprinkle in a little cornmeal, making sure to tilt and rotate the can so the meal covers the bottom and sides. Cornmeal makes a nice crust, too. This is a good trick to use with *any* kind of container you may have doubts about or whenever your dough is a sticky one.

When baking round loaves, you can use cake pans. Or, as long as the dough is stiff enough to hold its shape, you can use any type of flat baking pan—a cookie sheet, the bottom part of a broiler pan, or a large roasting pan, for example.

BOWLS

All standard yeast bread recipes tell you to mix the ingredients in a bowl and then turn the dough onto a floured board to knead—but I have always found that cleaning that awful board is the only part of bread baking that I really dislike. A board that is large enough to work on is usually too large to fit into the sink conveniently. It also manages, sneakily, to dump puddles of water all over the floor while I'm scrubbing away at the doughy remnants. When I've used a smaller board, the floor winds up covered with flour when I knead. It always seemed like a losing effort. Then I discovered a way to avoid using a board alto-

gether. Here is my *big secret:* I mix and then knead my dough in a round plastic dishpan.

A dishpan, which is roughly 13 inches in diameter, has sides that are about 6 inches high—high enough to keep the flour and dough inside, but low enough for your arms to reach over easily. It also has a large flat bottom that is perfect for kneading. Because it is made of plastic, a dishpan holds the heat well so the dough stays warm. Furthermore, it is just the right size to sit in the sink and soak itself clean. I even let the dough rise in this pan, so clean-up is minimal. This is the only piece of specialized equipment I urge you to buy. I bought mine in the supermarket, but you can also find one in discount stores like Kmart and Wal-Mart, as well as most hardware stores. (The Martha Stewart section in Kmart calls them "dish tubs.") Best of all, a dishpan requires only a very small investment, which will pay for itself many times over. If you cannot find one, you can use any large bowl or basin with similar dimensions. Or, if you prefer preparing your bread dough using a classical approach—or you are just plain stubborn (and don't mind additional cleanup)—go ahead and use a board.

You will also need to have a few standard mixing bowls on hand. They are necessary for preparing quick bread batters, as well as for combining various ingredients called for in different recipes.

ADDITIONAL ITEMS

Along with the basic equipment just mentioned, you'll need a wooden spoon, which I find best for mixing. I have also found that a plastic pot scraper is a useful tool for cleaning dough off your hands, as well as the dishpan, board, or bowl used to mix and knead the dough. When your bread comes out of the oven, you will want to cool it on a wire rack. And when it is ready to be sliced, a serrated bread knife is essential.

BASIC BREAD-MAKING METHOD

Earlier, I made the flat claim that it's easy to make yeast bread. Here are just a few of the things that *make* it easy:

■ You hardly ever have to measure the ingredients very carefully.

■ You never have to sift the flour.

■ You can let yeast dough sit around for a long time and nothing terrible will happen to it.

■ You can slam the oven door and the bread will not fall.

With this much latitude it isn't easy to make mistakes, but even if you do, you can nearly always correct them. Of course, it's helpful to have a good sense of what to expect as you create your delicious homemade loaves, as well as the recommended techniques for ensuring successful results. So let's take a detailed, step-by-step look at the bread-making process, including illustrations and helpful tips. We'll use the Basic White Bread recipe from Chapter 3 to serve as our model.

Keep in mind that the following method is certainly not the only one for yeast breads—ingredients, kneading times, baking temperatures, and loaf shapes will vary from recipe to recipe. It is, however, a standard, easy-to-follow procedure that, once mastered, will enable you to prepare all kinds of breads with confidence and ease.

TIP Almost all the yeast bread recipes in this book call for a variable amount of flour, such as four to six cups. This is because there is a tremendous difference in flours, which vary from brand to brand. Even a given brand may vary from batch to batch because it comes from different wheat crops. In addition, dough is strongly affected by temperature and humidity. The same recipe will require different amounts of flour on hot, humid days, than it does on cold, dry days. Occasionally, you may have to use even more than the maximum amount mentioned in the recipe. It's perfectly all right to do so as long as you add the additional flour slowly. You can always add more, but you can't take any out, so be very careful. Always add the minimum amount of flour first, then continue adding a little more at a time until you can handle the dough. Mix it with a wooden spoon until it becomes too stiff to stir, then switch to your hands.

BASIC WHITE BREAD

1 tablespoon (1 packet) active dry yeast

$2/3$ cup nonfat dry milk powder

1 tablespoon sugar

2 cups lukewarm water

3 tablespoons oil

1 tablespoon salt

5–6 cups unbleached white flour

Preparing the Dough

STEP 1. Put the yeast, milk powder, sugar, and warm water into a dishpan or large bowl. (For the sake of brevity and convenience, I'll simply say "bowl," but you'll know it's a dishpan, won't you?)

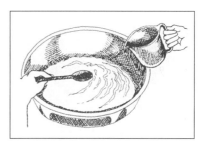

1. Add ingredients

STEP 2. Stir the ingredients with a wooden spoon, then add the salt, oil, and 3 cups of flour. Beat well with the spoon for about 2 minutes. Add 2 more cups of flour, then measure 1 more cup and set it aside so that you can add more flour later if necessary without making too much of a mess with your doughy hands. Speaking of doughy hands, this is a good time to put a plastic bag within easy reach so that you can slip your hand into it in case the phone rings. (It almost always does.)

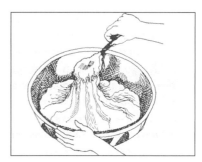

2. Stir

STEP 3. Plunge your hand into the bowl and mix and squeeze until all the flour disappears. If the dough is so wet that you can't pick up any part of it, add a little more flour. Dough is "ready to handle" when you can pick it up. At first, it should be like soft clay—very sticky, but not so wet that it sags through your fingers when you hold a handful. As soon as the dough is ready, stop adding flour. It's time to knead.

Kneading the Dough

3. Mix

STEP 4. If you are kneading right in your dishpan (and I hope you are), sprinkle a little flour on top of the dough and a little more on your hands, then scoop up the dough and turn it over. (If you find the dough impossible to turn over, it needs more flour.) At first the dough will be very sticky and cling to all your fingers in big globs. But after a few minutes, it will begin to stick to itself and start to feel smooth. If it remains hopelessly sticky, you will need to add more flour, but the trick is to add *just* enough and not too much. Press the dough down and away from your body with the heel of your hand (or hands). If you are using a board, dust it with flour before adding the dough, and then proceed in exactly the same way.

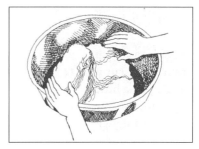

4. Knead

5. Fold

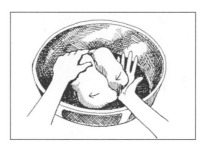

6. Turn

7. Knead

STEP 5. After a few strokes, fold the dough over from back to front and knead some more. When you pick up the back edge to fold it forward, sprinkle a tiny bit of flour on the exposed part of the pan or board if the dough sticks to it.

STEP 6. After a few folds and kneads, turn the lump of dough about a quarter of the way around.

STEP 7. Continue to knead, fold, and turn for anywhere from four to ten minutes—even longer if the recipe calls for it. Since there are variations in flours, temperatures, and humidity (as well as kneaders), readiness should not be judged by the clock, but by the feel and look of the dough. It should be elastic and springy, like a soft rubber ball (and no longer stick to your hands). When you press it, it will fight back. It will also develop a smooth, satiny look and may have little blisters on its surface. Keep in mind that whole grain doughs will not be as smooth (and probably not as shiny) as those made with white flour, so you'll have to depend on the bouncy, springy feel as a sign that you've kneaded enough.

TIP There is more than one way to knead dough, and with a little practice you will develop your own style. You can knead with one hand and switch to the other when the first hand gets tired, or you can knead with both hands at once. Do whatever feels comfortable, and work on a surface that is low enough for you to put your body weight behind your arms. Unless you are extremely tall, you might find kitchen counters too high for kneading, so try a table.

> **TIP** I have found the best place for dough to rise is in the oven (one that is not turned on, of course). If you have a gas oven with a pilot light, first check to make sure the oven isn't too warm (it should be well under 100°F) and simply place the covered bowl inside. If there is no pilot light, leave on the oven's electric light bulb. And if there is no light bulb, set a pan of hot water in the bottom of the oven. The heavy insulation of the oven walls will keep in the heat for a long time. If you can't tie up the oven, you will have to find another warm spot. Since heat rises, a high shelf in a kitchen cupboard or the top of the refrigerator are both good places. And if the weather is hot and the kitchen is warm, you can simply leave the bowl right on the counter.

STEP 8. Now you can easily form the dough into a ball. When you pick it up and hold it in one hand, if it holds its shape, it's time for the first rising.

Letting the Dough Rise

STEP 9. If you are using a dishpan to mix and knead the dough, you can also let the dough rise in it. You do not have to wash the pan, but do remove any excess flour and scrape away any scraps of dry dough that may be lurking on the bottom or sides. Pick up the ball of dough, then pour a little oil (about a teaspoonful) into the pan and spread it around the bottom and up the sides. Place the dough back in the oiled bowl, then turn the dough over so the oily side is on top. Cover the bowl with plastic wrap or a clean dishtowel and set it in a warm spot so the yeast will grow quickly and cause the dough to rise.

STEP 10. Recipes usually tell you to let the dough rise until it has "doubled in bulk," which generally takes about an hour or so. This may, however, be a little hard to judge by simply looking at the dough. So when you think it has risen enough, stick one or two fingers (up to the first joint) into the risen dough. If the hole remains when you take your fingers out, the dough has risen enough.

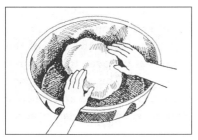

8. Shape

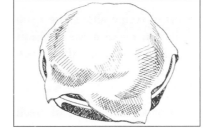

9. Cover

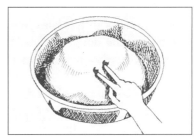

10. Poke

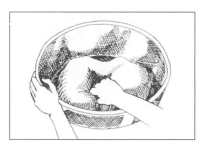

11. Punch

Punching Down the Dough

STEP 11. Once the dough has risen, it's time to "punch it down." That's right, it's time to take your floured fist, and bury it in that swollen ball of dough, which is now filled with gas bubbles. Punching it is like puncturing a balloon—the gas escapes and the dough deflates. After it flattens, fold the dough over a few times and press it down with the palms of your hands to force out any remaining gas.

Shaping the Loaves

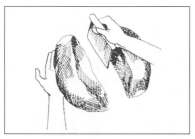

12. Cut

STEP 12. Shape the dough into a ball and cut it in half with a sharp knife or dough cutter. (Although the dough can be shaped into rounds or free-formed loaves that are baked on a flat baking sheet, in this example, it will be made into two loaves and baked in standard 9-x-5-inch loaf pans.)

STEP 13. Press each piece of dough into a flattened rectangle (right in the bowl or on a floured board) that is a little longer than the pan. Starting with one of the long sides, roll the dough tightly and pinch the seam together.

13. Roll

STEP 14. Turn the loaf over so that the seam is on the bottom, and then tuck the ends under neatly. Don't worry if the loaf is smaller than the pan because it has to rise again, and when it does, it will fill up any extra space.

STEP 15. Place the loaves in well-greased (with oil or butter) 9-x-5-inch loaf pans.

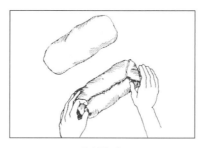

14. Tuck

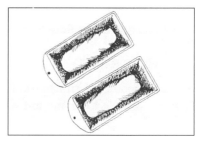

15. Place

> **TIP** At first, the term "fold" may not have much meaning. Even though you can bend the mass of dough over itself, it hardly makes a neat fold; but as you keep working and the gluten starts to develop, the dough will begin to hold its shape nicely. It will even stop sticking in huge globs to your fingers. If this doesn't happen within a few minutes, shake in a little more flour. In a very short time you will get the "feel" of when the dough is just right.)

Letting the Dough Rise Again

STEP 16. When the loaves have been shaped, it is time for the second rising. Cover the pans with plastic wrap or a clean towel and return them to a warm spot to rise again. This second rising usually takes only about half as long the first. Once the loaves have risen, it's time to bake them. Unless otherwise specified, preheat the oven as directed, which, for this recipe is 400°F.

16. Wait

Baking the Loaves

STEP 17. While the oven is heating up, use a sharp knife or single-edge razor blade to cut a few $\frac{1}{2}$-inch-deep slits into the top of the dough to let the steam escape as it bakes. The slits will also spread apart during baking to make a decorative pattern. For long loaves, you can make three or four diagonal slits, or one long slit down the center. For round loaves, cut a cross or a few diagonal slits on top. A tic-tac-toe with two slits in each direction also makes an interesting top on round loaves.

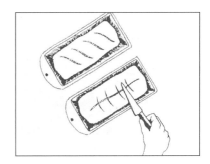
17. Score

STEP 18. For a crisp crust, brush the tops of the loaves with cold water (use a pastry brush, a spray bottle, or your fingers) just before popping them into the oven. If you want a *very* crisp crust, repeat this cold-water treatment once or twice more during the baking period. You can also place a pan of hot water on the bottom of the oven or toss in a few ice cubes to create steam, which makes for a good crust. If you prefer a soft crust, brush the tops of the loaves with butter or oil before baking. Brush on more as soon as they come out of the oven.

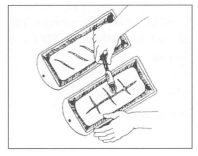
18. Brush

TIP For a round or oval loaf, mold the dough into a ball by cupping your hands around it, while frequently slapping it down and turning. For a long bread, like a French baguette or an Italian-style loaf, use the same technique as for a loaf-pan bread, only make a much longer, narrower rectangle. To bake bread in a coffee can, clay pot, or other unorthodox container, just form the dough into roughly the same shape as the container and drop it in. And if you are going to bake your bread on a flat pan or baking sheet, you can form it into any shape you want.

You can vary these basic shapes to create loaves with different, more interesting looks. For instance, when you make a round bread, save a small piece of dough, form it into a ball, and set it on top—right in the center—of the larger round. This adds a decorative touch to the basic round loaf. When making a long bread, turn it into a spiral by giving the dough a twist. Make braided breads by dividing the dough into three strands, rolling them with your hands into ropes, and then braiding them together. You can also make patterned breads by baking them in special molds, such as bundt pans. Be creative and enjoy the experience.

19. Rap

STEP 19. Place the pans in the oven on a fairly low shelf. The top of the baked bread should reach the center of the oven (roughly). If you are using more than one pan, do not let them touch each other or the sides of the oven. Use a timer or watch the clock as a guide for baking doneness, but keep in mind that this will give you only an approximate indication. For a true test of doneness, turn the bread out of the pan (or remove it from the baking sheet) and rap it on the bottom with your knuckle. It should make a hollow sound. If it doesn't, put it back in the oven (in or out of the pan), bake it a few minutes more, and then try again. If the bottom of the bread isn't brown enough, don't put it back in the pan; place it directly on the oven rack to bake a little longer.

20. Cool

STEP 20. As soon as you remove the bread from the oven, turn it out of the pan and place it right side up or on its side on a wire rack to cool. If you leave hot bread on a solid surface, the bottom will get soggy from the steam that is created. If you do not have a rack, place the bread crosswise on a loaf pan or bowl so the air can circulate all around it. If you can wait that long, let the bread cool until you can handle it comfortably, then slice it with a serrated knife.

TIP Although the heat of the oven will kill the yeast and stop the rising process, there will be some delay before it penetrates to the center of the loaf. This means you can expect some further rising during the first few minutes of baking.

Emergency Procedures and Diagnoses

Even though it seems as if you've done everything right, you may find that your bread is too soggy or lumpy or pale. Maybe in the middle of preparing the dough, you run into a snag. What follows are some common "challenges" that can occur during bread making and their suggested solutions.

■ If you are interrupted while in the middle of preparing dough for yeast bread, don't worry about it. If the interruption is a phone call, just cover the dough to keep it from drying out (and don't stay on the phone too long). If someone invites you to play two sets of tennis while the dough is rising, punch it down, cover it with plastic wrap, and put it in the refrigerator until you get back. If someone invites you to Paris for a month, wrap the dough and put it in the freezer. In each of these cases, you will be able to pick up just where you left off. (These rules do *not* apply to quick breads, which can be set aside before the leavening has been added, but *must* be baked promptly once it has.)

■ Dough that rises either too much or too quickly results in bread with a coarse texture. If you forget to keep an eye on the dough while it's rising (even if it is already in a pan) and it much more than doubles in bulk, punch it down and let it rise again. Only this time, *do* watch it; and be aware that it will rise much faster the second time. Actually, multiple risings result in bread with a fine texture, so you might actually want to do this at times.

■ If your dough does not rise at all, it means that either the yeast was dead when you started, or you killed it with liquid that was too hot. Unfortunately, the only thing you can do is begin again; but before you do, be sure to test (prove) the yeast to make sure it is still active. Mix a tablespoon of yeast in one-quarter cup of lukewarm water and add a few grains of sugar. If the mixture becomes foamy within five to ten minutes, the yeast is alive and well, and you can use it. (Also make sure to use lukewarm liquid to form the dough.) When proofing, if the mixture does not foam, the yeast is past its prime. Discard it and buy a fresh supply.

■ If you add more flour than your dough can absorb, dump out the excess. Then work a little water into the dough, a few drops at a time.

■ If your bread has lumps, you didn't mix the dough thoroughly enough. Next time, be sure to beat in part of the flour before adding the last few cups, and always scrape the sides and bottom of the bowl well. If you find any dry scraps of dough clinging to the bowl or board, throw them away. Don't try to work them in.

■ If your bread is pale and damp, you didn't bake it enough. Put it back in the oven—even if you have already cut it—for another fifteen to twenty minutes.

■ If the bread is soggy, you might have used too much liquid or, to put it another way, not enough flour. Bread also becomes soggy if it is put into an airtight container before it has thoroughly cooled.

■ If the bread starts to get very brown as it bakes, but still has a lot of baking time left, lay a piece of aluminum foil over the top. If your oven browns unevenly (as many do) shift the pans around during the middle of the baking period. Unlike cake, bread does not fall as it bakes, so it's all right to move it.

STORING BREAD

Although there's a good chance that your beautiful freshly baked loaves will be eaten quickly without a crumb to spare, there is always the possibility of leftovers. Or if you have made more than one loaf, you might plan to serve one today and save the other (or others) to enjoy tomorrow. Keep in mind that bread gets stale because it loses its moisture; but contrary to what most people think, it does so faster in the refrigerator than at room temperature. I have found the best way to keep bread fresher longer is by keeping it in a breadbox or a cloth bag at room temperature. My next (although less-desirable) method for storing bread is to place it in a plastic bag. If you do this with a crispy loaf, the crust will become soft; however, you can crisp it up by placing it in a hot oven for a few minutes. Bread can also get moldy quickly in warm, humid weather; so under these conditions you'll have no choice but to bag or wrap it and then place it in the refrigerator. I find the best plan is always to keep out just enough for immediate use and freeze the rest.

All types of bread, including quick breads and muffins, freeze well. Simply wrap your homemade loaves securely in aluminum foil, then seal them in plastic bags, making sure to press out all the air before closing the bags. You must also make sure to let the bread cool *thoroughly* before wrapping it up. If you don't, ice crystals will form inside the wrapper and the bread will become soggy as it thaws. To reheat frozen bread, leave it in its foil wrapper and place in a moderately warm oven (around 350°F or so), for about fifteen to twenty minutes, or until it feels soft. Remove the foil and leave the bread in the oven another few minutes to crisp the crust. Do not heat your bread in the microwave; it will become rubbery.

HIGH-ALTITUDE BAKING

If you live in a high-altitude location (over 3,000 feet), there is one more important consideration. Due to the area's low air pressure, the carbon dioxide gas will rise more than it does at sea level. This is likely to cause the dough to stretch too much and result in a coarse-textured bread. To prevent this from happening, you'll have to make a leavening adjustment. You can either reduce the amount of yeast, and use about one-fourth less than the amount called for, or you can let the dough rise twice (instead of once) before shaping the loaves, punching it down each time. For quick breads, reduce the baking powder or baking soda by one-fourth the amount called for in the recipe.

And there they are—my recommended techniques and suggested guidelines for baking yeast bread. Now close your eyes and imagine the experience. . . . Picture yourself putting your hands into the warm, soft dough, while focusing on the beautiful Zen experience of creating something with your hands; feeling the dough change, come alive, as you work it; seeing it turn smooth and satiny as you coax it into form; then placing the loaves in the oven, and letting them fill the house with a heartwarming mouth-watering aroma. Next, imagine cutting your bread and handing a still-warm-from-the-oven slice to someone you love. Baking bread will fill your heart with peace and joy.

HELPFUL TIPS BEFORE YOU BEGIN

By now, you are probably anxious to dig your hands into that silky flour and begin making your own wonderful bread. But wait just another moment or two. Although you are armed with the bread-making basics, before you actually begin, there are still a few more details you are sure to find helpful. Over many years of making homemade breads, I have discovered a number of helpful tips and bits of information—in addition to the valuable emergency procedures found in the inset on page 25—that I'd like to share with you.

❑ To help you judge the amount of flour to buy, one pound yields about $3\frac{3}{4}$ cups.

❑ You can cut any of my bread recipes in half by simply halving the amount of each ingredient, with one exception: the yeast. If the original directions call for only one packet or one tablespoon of yeast, use it all, even though you are halving everything else. If the directions call for *two or more* packets of yeast, only then can you cut the amount in half.

❑ Measurements for yeast bread ingredients never have to be exact, as they do for cakes. Make a reasonable effort to be accurate, but don't bother to level off exact cups of flour with the edge of a knife or spatula. Since large quantities of flour are often used, it saves time (and prevents you from losing count) to use a large measuring cup. Just dip it into the canister or sack.

❑ Never sift flour for yeast bread. And although many cookbooks require sifted flour for quick breads, this one does not. If you want to sift, go ahead, but I have never been able to perceive that it has made any difference.

❑ Before kneading, scrub your hands and nails with a hand brush and remove your rings. You will find this useful after kneading, too.

❑ Earlier in this chapter, you learned that brushing the loaf with cold water before baking results in a crisp crust. If you would also like a crisp crust with a glaze, brush with a slightly beaten egg white mixed with 1 tablespoon of cold water. Repeat once or twice during baking.

❑ For very, very soft crust, brush the tops of the loaves with butter or oil before baking and repeat as soon as you remove them from the oven. Wrap the loaves in plastic wrap while they are still slightly warm.

❑ Breads made with oil or butter stay fresh longer than those made without fat.

❑ You can always substitute butter for oil in a bread recipe (except when the recipe calls for olive oil) if you prefer. Melt the butter first and let it cool to lukewarm. Always measure the butter *after* it is melted.

❑ A word on storing dough: Since all bread is best when freshly baked, you may want to mix a batch of dough and bake only part of it. Place the unused dough in a zippered plastic bag and store it in the refrigerator, where it will keep for several days. The dough may continue to rise a very little bit even at refrigerator temperature, so leave room in the bag and keep an eye on it. If the dough appears to grow, punch it down, then store it again. Dough will keep in an airtight plastic bag for several weeks in the freezer. When you're ready, simply thaw it, then pick up the procedure wherever you left off.

❑ Although it is a great temptation to cut bread as soon as it comes out of the oven, most breads cut and taste better if you let them cool somewhat first. Use a serrated knife for slicing.

❑ You can greatly increase the protein value of white flour by doing the following: Every time you measure one cup of flour, first put one tablespoon each of soy flour, wheat germ, and nonfat dry milk powder into the cup, and then add the flour. This mixture is called *Cornell flour,* named after the university where it was developed by Dr. Clive M. McCay and his coworkers.

❑ Don't be afraid to experiment. You can add chopped nuts, cheese, raisins, currants, a little leftover cooked cereal or rice, a bit of mashed potato, herbs, saffron, or just about any ingredient to most bread doughs. For added flavor, try using use fruit juice or the liquid from cooked vegetables instead of water.

Remember, no matter what you do, the odds are against your bread coming out exactly the same way twice; but that's part of the excitement. Don't reject your bread just because it's different from the last one you made. Although it may not be precisely what you expected, it is probably very good—and possibly even better than you had imagined.

TIME TO BEGIN

If you have never baked bread before, a great new experience lies ahead—and don't be anxious about it. Baking bread is easy! Even if your first loaf doesn't look exactly like the picture in the book (it might look better), it's almost impossible to have a failure. Bread is always unique, and it's almost always good. It's *hard* to ruin bread, which is, without a doubt, one of the secrets of its long-lasting success. Think about all the different kinds of people who have baked different kinds of breads under all sorts of conditions over thousands and thousands of years. If they could do it, so can you.

Furthermore, the information in this chapter has armed you with everything you need to create the delectable array of breads found in the following chapters. Whether you choose to make yeast breads or quick breads, flatbreads or muffins, you know the best ingredients, the right tools and utensils, and the proper techniques for ensuring successful results. Now that you are prepared for just about anything, it's time to bake bread.

PART TWO

THE RECIPES

3. Mostly White Breads

White bread, the most familiar kind, is a recent arrival in the story of bread. For centuries, early people made coarse breads of barley, millet, and other seeds that had been crushed between stones. And even when the Egyptians learned to make ground wheat flour around 3000 BC, the flour was brown because it contained bran. Those who could afford it, shook their flour through sieves to produce a fairly white flour and the rough bran that remained in the sieve was either discarded or given to the servants. But by the late seventeenth century, some white flour became commercially available in Europe—particularly in France—and it quickly became a status symbol that was highly prized

During the 1770s, steam-powered roller mills were producing fine Hungarian-process white flour, and the first really important flour mill in the United States was opened in Minneapolis in 1878. White bread became the staple bread of Americans, and it's easy to understand why. Made with refined flour, white breads are lighter and airier than any whole grain bread can ever be. They have a soft texture and a tender crumb, and to people who had

been accustomed to coarser whole grain breads, that softness quickly became the symbol of luxury and refinement.

The appeal of white bread was not just in the eating, but in the making, as well. For the home baker, the new, fine white flour was more "user-friendly" than the older, coarser kind. It made a white dough that was easy to knead, quick to bake, and yielded a dependable, delicious loaf every time.

Making white bread today is virtually foolproof, and a basic recipe lends itself to great variety. With the addition of some semolina flour to the basic white bread dough, you can make delicious Semolina Bread with a flavor and "feel" unlike any other; add some mashed potatoes to the basic recipe and enjoy Roadside Potato Bread, an old-fashioned American farmhouse bread with a sensuous texture; or use a dash of olive oil and a hint of rosemary to recreate the taste of Italy in Rosemary-Olive Oil Bread. You can make many kinds of basically white breads by adding your own selection of herbs and spices, fruits and nuts, and even cheese; you can also vary the shapes of your loaves and your baking methods.

The most popular breads of all—based on their enduring popularity—are the old standards: Basic White Bread, baked in a loaf pan and so familiar to Americans, is excellent for slicing, for sandwiches, and for toast; French Bread, with its classic baguette form, airy interior, and crispy crust, is a favorite dinner bread, especially suited to being broken into chunks and used to mop up sauce. Another favorite is Cuban Bread, similar to Mediterranean-style breads and one that you can whip up in record time. You will find recipes for these and other delicious white breads in the pages that follow. Detailed steps for the Basic Bread-Making procedure are found in Chapter 2, beginning on page 18.

BASIC WHITE BREAD

Considered "basic" because it can serve as the basis for many other breads, this standard loaf keeps well and is very versatile. It can be used to make sandwiches or toast, enjoyed as an accompaniment to meals, or simply eaten by itself. It also makes fine bread crumbs. The method for making this bread is basic, too (see pages 18–24 for a detailed version). Once you have made it, you will be able to make just about any bread with confidence.

YIELD: 2 LARGE LOAVES

1 tablespoon (1 packet) active dry yeast

1 tablespoon sugar

2/3 cup nonfat dry milk powder

2 cups lukewarm water

1 tablespoon salt

3 tablespoons oil

5–6 cups unbleached white flour

1. Place the yeast, sugar, milk powder, and water in a dishpan or large bowl and stir with a wooden spoon. Add the salt, oil, and 3 cups of flour. Beat with the spoon for 2 minutes.

2. Add 2 more cups of flour, stir in as much as you can, then squeeze the mixture with your hands until the flour disappears. If it is too wet to pick up, add a little more flour. As soon as you can handle the dough, sprinkle with a bit more flour and begin to knead directly in the bowl (or on a floured board), adding more flour as necessary. Knead for 8 to10 minutes, or until the dough feels smooth and elastic. Shape into a ball.

3. Spread a little oil on the bottom and sides of the bowl. Add the ball of dough, then turn it over, oiled side up. Cover and set in a warm spot for about an hour, or until the dough doubles in bulk. Thoroughly grease (with oil or butter) two 9-x-5-inch bread pans and set aside.

4. Punch down the risen dough and form into a ball. Cut in half, knead for a minute or so, and pat each half into a flattened rectangle that is a little longer than the pans. Starting at one of the long sides, tightly roll up each rectangle. Pinch the seam together, turn the loaf over, and tuck the ends under neatly. Place seam-side down in the prepared pans, cover, and let rise for 30 minutes, or until doubled in bulk (the loaves will just about reach the top of the pans).

5. Cut two or more $1/2$-inch-deep slashes across the top of each risen loaf. For a crisp crust, brush with cold water; for a soft crust, brush with a little soft butter or oil. Place in a preheated 400°F oven and bake for about 35 minutes, or until the loaves are browned and hollow-sounding when rapped on the bottom with your knuckle. Cool on a wire rack before serving.

VARIATIONS

Unless otherwise noted, all additions to this recipe should be made before the dough is kneaded. If you make a late decision, knead in the extra ingredients just before shaping the loaves, and make sure they are well distributed.

Dill Bread Add 4 tablespoons fresh chopped dill, or 2 tablespoons dried.

Mixed Herb Bread Add 1 teaspoon each of dried basil, thyme, and oregano. You can also use 1 tablespoon of any one herb if you prefer.

Orange-Nut Bread Omit the milk powder and warm water, and substitute 2 cups lukewarm orange juice. Add 1 cup seedless raisins or currants, and $1/2$ cup chopped walnuts or pecans.

Light Rye Bread Substitute 2 cups rye flour for 2 cups of the white flour.

Cinnamon-Raisin Bread Add 1 cup seedless raisins and 2 teaspoons cinnamon. For slightly sweeter bread, increase the sugar to $1/4$ cup.

Cheese Bread Omit the sugar. Add 1 extra tablespoon oil (a total of 4) and 1 cup grated or shredded Cheddar or Gruyère cheese. You can also make this bread using all or part grated Parmesan. Bake at 375°F, and check for doneness after 30 minutes.

Light Wheat Germ Bread Add 1 cup wheat germ before adding any flour.

ENGLISH COTTAGE BREAD

*This very simple but attractive white bread has a good texture
and crisp crust. When cut into large slices, it is particularly
suitable for open-face sandwiches (or really hefty closed ones).
You can copy this shape for any kind of bread.*

**YIELD:
2 MEDIUM ROUNDS**

2 tablespoons (2 packets)
 active dry yeast

2 cups lukewarm water

1 tablespoon salt

6–7 cups unbleached
 white flour

1. Place the yeast and water in a dishpan or large bowl, and stir with a wooden spoon. Add the salt and 4 cups of flour, and beat with the spoon until well blended.

2. Add 2 more cups of flour, then squeeze the mixture with your hands until the flour disappears. If it is too wet to pick up, add a little more flour. As soon as you can handle the dough, sprinkle with a bit more flour and begin to knead directly in the bowl (or on a floured board), adding more flour as necessary. Knead for about 5 to 7 minutes, or until the dough feels smooth and elastic. Shape into a ball.

3. Spread a little oil on the bottom and sides of the bowl. Add the ball of dough, then turn it over, oiled side up. Cover and set in a warm spot for about an hour, or until the dough doubles in bulk. Grease a large baking sheet and set aside.

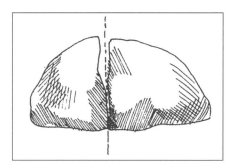

Divide the dough in half.

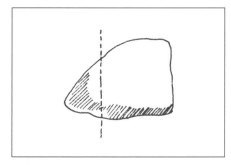

Cut a small piece from each half.

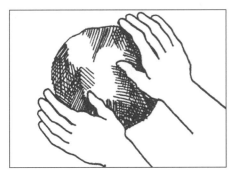

Shape the pieces into balls.

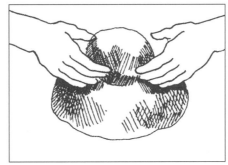

Place a small ball of dough on a large one.

4. Punch down the risen dough, knead for a minute or so, then form into a ball. Cut in half. As shown in the figure on page 34, cut off a small piece (about a third) from each half. Shape the two larger pieces into balls, flatten them very slightly, and place on the prepared baking sheet, leaving enough space between them to allow for expansion. Form the smaller pieces into slightly flattened balls, and center them on top of the larger ones. Flour your index finger and push it all the way through the center of both balls. Cover the loaves and let rise about 30 minutes, or until doubled in bulk.

5. Place the risen loaves in a preheated 400°F oven. After 30 minutes, reduce the heat to 375°F and bake for about another 20 minutes, or until the loaves are very brown and hollow-sounding when rapped on the bottom with your knuckle. Cool on a wire rack before serving.

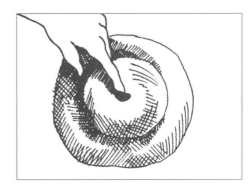

Push your finger through the center of both balls.

FRENCH BREAD

This is one of my favorite French bread recipes. Fairly quick and easy, it produces long, thin delicious loaves with a crisp, crunchy crust. To achieve the proper texture, the dough should be kneaded for a long time. To minimize the labor, you can use an electric mixer to do some of the beating in Step 1. See the inset on page 37 for more information on French bread.

YIELD: 4 LONG THIN LOAVES

- 2 tablespoons (2 packets) active dry yeast
- 3 cups lukewarm water
- 1½ tablespoons salt
- 7–8 cups unbleached white flour
- 1 egg white plus 1 tablespoon cold water
- 1–2 tablespoons cornmeal for the baking sheet

1. Place the yeast, water, salt, and 3 cups of flour in a large bowl, and beat well with a wooden spoon or an electric mixer at medium speed. Add another 2 cups of flour and continue beating for 2 minutes.

2. Add 2 more cups of flour, then squeeze the mixture with your hands until the flour disappears. If it is too wet to pick up, add a little more flour. As soon as you can handle the dough, sprinkle with a bit more flour and begin to knead directly in the bowl (or on a floured board). Knead for 8 to 10 minutes, or until the dough feels smooth and elastic. Shape into a ball.

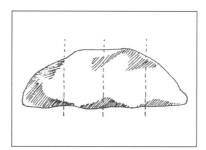

Divide the dough into fourths.

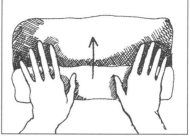

Flatten each piece into a rectangle.

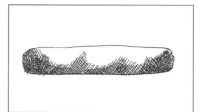

Roll up each piece tightly.

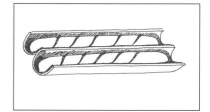

Place in baguette pans or on a baking sheet.

3. Spread a little oil on the bottom and sides of the bowl. Add the ball of dough, then turn it over, oiled side up. Cover and set in a warm spot for about an hour, or until the dough doubles in bulk. Lightly sprinkle a large baking sheet with cornmeal and set aside.

4. Punch down the risen dough, knead for a minute, and form into a ball. Cut into four equal pieces, and pat each piece into a long flattened rectangle that is almost the length of the baking sheet. Starting at one of the long sides, tightly roll up each rectangle. Pinch the seam together, turn the loaf over, and tuck the ends under neatly. Place the loaves seam-side down on the baking sheet, leaving enough space between them to allow for expansion. Cover and let rise about 30 minutes, or until doubled in bulk.

5. Cut several $1/2$-inch-deep diagonal slashes across the top of each risen loaf. In a small bowl, beat together the egg white and cold water, then brush some on each loaf (for a very crisp crust).

6. Place the loaves in a cold oven, and set a pan of very hot water on the bottom (to create steam as the bread bakes). Turn on the oven to 400°F and bake for 35 to 40 minutes, or until the loaves are nicely browned and hollow-sounding when rapped on the bottom with your knuckle. Serve hot from the oven (break it, don't slice it), or after cooling on a wire rack.

French Bread—*C'est Magnifique!*

All over France, one can see long, long loaves of bread sticking out of string bags, tied to the backs of bicycles, or clutched in the arms of children not much taller than the loaves themselves. Because these baguettes are best enjoyed fresh from the oven, it is customary to buy a fresh loaf for every meal.

When the term "French bread" appears in a recipe intended for home use, it is a misnomer; "French-style bread" is more accurate. Real French bakery bread—that most superb of loaves with its crunchy crust and light-as-air interior—is impossible to duplicate in your kitchen, largely because of oven limitations. Commercial ovens that turn out authentic French bread reach much higher temperatures than home ovens, and the heat comes from all sides, not just the bottom. They also emit steam, which helps give French bread its characteristic crisp crust.

Authentic French baguettes are also *very* long;

however, your oven is probably not wide enough to fit pans of this length. You'll have to shape the loaves to fit your pans and your oven. You can use U-shaped baguette pans, which come in various lengths and are often attached in pairs, or you can hand shape the dough into long thin loaves and bake them on a flat baking sheet. Setting a pan of water in the bottom of the oven creates steam, which helps crisp the crust as the bread bakes (you can also toss a few ice cubes into the hot oven, or spray water on the oven walls for similar "steamy" results). And keep in mind that French bread does not keep for more than a day, so freeze any freshly baked loaves that you don't plan to eat right away. (Freezing directions are on page 26.)

Whether split down the middle for sandwiches or served as an accompaniment to meals (especially for mopping up sauce or gravy), French bread—commercial or homemade—is always a treat.

GREEN BREAD

*This very attractive, tangy bread isn't **really** green. It takes its name from the profusion of finely chopped green herbs it contains. If using fresh herbs instead of dried, be sure to double the quantity. You can experiment with flavor changes by substituting dill or rosemary for the tarragon.*

YIELD: 2 LARGE ROUNDS

2 tablespoons (2 packets) active dry yeast

2 cups lukewarm water

4 tablespoons honey

7–8 cups unbleached white flour

1 1/2 tablespoons salt

4 tablespoons oil

3 eggs

1/2 cup finely chopped fresh parsley

1 teaspoon dried basil

1 teaspoon dried tarragon

Pinch cinnamon (about 1/4 teaspoon)

1 egg white plus 1 tablespoon cold water

1. Place the yeast, water, and honey in a dishpan or large bowl. Add 3 cups of flour and beat well with a wooden spoon until the batter is perfectly smooth. Cover and set in a warm place for about an hour, or until the yeast batter (sponge) has doubled in bulk.

2. Stir the batter, then beat in the salt, oil, eggs, parsley, basil, and tarragon (rub the dried herbs between your fingers to powder them before adding). Add the cinnamon and 4 more cups of the flour, then squeeze the mixture with your hands until the flour disappears. If it is too wet to pick up, add a little more flour. As soon as you can handle the dough, sprinkle with a bit more flour and begin to knead directly in the bowl (or on a floured board), adding more flour as necessary. Knead for 10 minutes, or until the dough feels smooth and elastic. Shape into a ball.

3. Spread a little oil on the bottom and sides of the bowl. Add the ball of dough, then turn it over, oiled side up. Cover and set in a warm spot for about an hour, or until the dough doubles in bulk. Punch down the dough, and let it rise a second time until doubled in bulk again. Grease a large baking sheet and set aside.

4. After the second rising, punch down the dough again, knead for a minute, and form into a ball. Cut in half. As shown in the figure on page 34, cut off a small piece (about a third) from each half. Shape the two larger pieces into balls, flatten them very slightly, and place on the prepared baking sheet, leaving enough space between them to allow for expansion. Form the smaller pieces into slightly flattened balls, and set them on top of the larger ones. Cover the loaves and let rise 20 to 30 minutes, or until doubled in bulk.

5. In a small bowl, beat together the egg white and cold water, then brush some on each loaf. Place in a preheated 375°F oven and bake for 35 minutes, or until the loaves are as brown as old mahogany and hollow-sounding when rapped on the bottom with your knuckle. Cool on a wire rack before serving.

TOMATO-BASIL BREAD

A pleasant tomato flavor and piquant hint of basil makes this salmon-colored bread with its shiny, rosy-hued crust particularly lovely to serve with a crisp green salad. It's also an excellent choice for meat or cheese sandwiches.

1. Heat the tomato juice and butter in a small saucepan over low heat until just lukewarm. Remove from the heat and stir until the butter is melted. If the mixture is more than lukewarm, be sure to let it cool, then place it in a dishpan or large bowl along with the yeast, salt, basil, sugar, and 2 cups of flour. Beat well with a wooden spoon until perfectly smooth.

2. Continue to add flour, squeezing the mixture with your hands until you can handle the dough. Begin to knead directly in the bowl (or on a floured board), adding more flour as necessary. Knead for 5 minutes, or until the dough feels smooth and elastic. Shape into a ball.

3. Spread a little oil on the bottom and sides of the bowl. Add the ball of dough, then turn it over, oiled side up. Cover and set in a warm spot for about an hour, or until the dough doubles in bulk. Thoroughly grease (with oil or butter) two 8-x-4-inch bread pans and set aside.

4. Punch down the risen dough, knead a minute to eliminate any air bubbles, and form into a ball. Cut in half, and pat each half into a flattened rectangle that is a little longer than the pans. Starting at one of the long sides, tightly roll up each rectangle. Pinch the seam together, turn the loaf over, and tuck the ends under neatly. Place seam-side down in the prepared pans, cover, and let rise for about 30 minutes, or until doubled in bulk.

5. Cut two or more $\frac{1}{2}$-inch-deep slashes across the top of each risen loaf. In a small bowl, beat together the egg white and cold water, then brush some on each loaf (for a very crisp crust), and sprinkle with basil. Place in a preheated 375°F oven for 30 minutes, or until the loaves are very brown and hollow-sounding when rapped on the bottom with your knuckle. Cool on a wire rack before serving.

**YIELD:
2 MEDIUM LOAVES**

2 cups tomato juice

2 tablespoons butter

1 tablespoon (1 packet) active dry yeast

1 tablespoon salt

4 teaspoons finely chopped fresh basil, or 2 teaspoons dried

2 tablespoons sugar

5–7 cups unbleached white flour

1 egg white plus 1 tablespoon water

Chopped basil to sprinkle on loaves

CUBAN BREAD

When I need fresh bread in a hurry, this is the one I always choose. Similar to French and other Mediterranean-style breads, Cuban Bread is fast and easy to make (its second rising takes place as it bakes). This recipe traditionally calls for white flour only, but I find that using a combination of white and whole wheat flour gives it added flavor and character. When making this bread with white flour only, use 5 to 6 cups.

YIELD: 2 MEDIUM LOAVES

2 tablespoons (2 packets) active dry yeast

2 cups whole wheat flour

3–4 cups unbleached white flour

2 tablespoons sugar

1 tablespoon salt

2 cups lukewarm water

1–2 tablespoons cornmeal for the baking sheet

1. Place the yeast, whole wheat flour, 2 cups of white flour, sugar, and salt in a dishpan or large bowl. Add the water while stirring with a wooden spoon. Beat well with the spoon for 2 minutes.

2. Add 1 more cup of white flour, then squeeze the mixture with your hands until the flour disappears. If it is too wet to pick up, add a little more flour. As soon as you can handle the dough, sprinkle with a bit more flour and begin to knead directly in the bowl (or on a floured board), adding more flour as necessary. Knead for 5 to 6 minutes, or until the dough feels smooth and elastic. Shape into a ball.

3. Spread a little oil on the bottom and sides of the bowl. Add the ball of dough, then turn it over, oiled side up. Cover and set in a warm spot for about 15 minutes, or until the dough doubles in bulk. Lightly sprinkle a large baking sheet with cornmeal and set aside.

4. Punch down the risen dough, knead for a minute, and form into a ball. Cut in half, then pat each half into a torpedo-shaped loaf with a fat middle and gently tapered ends. Place the loaves on the prepared baking sheet, leaving enough space between them to allow for expansion.

5. Cut a $\frac{1}{2}$-inch-deep slash lengthwise down the center of each loaf. Brush the tops with cold water and place in a cold oven. (For a very crunchy crust, set a pan with very hot water in the bottom of the oven to create steam as the bread bakes.) Turn on the oven to 400°F and bake for 50 minutes, or until the loaves are brown, crisp, and hollow-sounding when rapped on the bottom with your knuckle. Cool on a wire rack before serving.

ROADSIDE POTATO BREAD

What roadsides have to do with this fine, tender bread with its excellent crust and moist, dense crumb is a mystery, but it always seems to be labeled with this quaint name. It's a good bread to bake in big round casseroles or metal coffee cans (just be sure they're well greased, dusted with cornmeal, and filled no more than halfway with dough). If using conventional loaf pans, oil or butter them and skip the cornmeal.

1. Place the potatoes, yeast, honey, water, milk powder, oil, and salt in a dishpan or large bowl and stir with a wooden spoon. Add 6 cups of flour and beat with the spoon until well blended.

2. Add 2 more cups of flour, then squeeze the mixture with your hands until the flour disappears. If it is too wet to pick up, add a little more flour. As soon as you can handle the dough, sprinkle with a bit more flour and begin to knead directly in the bowl (or on a floured board), adding more flour as necessary. Knead 5 to 7 minutes, or until the dough feels smooth and elastic. Shape into a ball.

3. Spread a little oil on the bottom and sides of the bowl. Add the ball of dough, then turn it over, oiled side up. Cover and set in a warm spot for at least an hour, or until the dough doubles in bulk. Punch down the dough, and let it rise a second time for about 40 minutes, or until doubled in bulk again. Thoroughly grease (with oil or butter) two 9-x-5-inch bread pans and set aside.

4. After the second rising, punch down the dough again, knead a minute to eliminate any air bubbles, and form into a ball. Cut in half, and pat each piece into a flattened rectangle that is a little longer than the pans. Starting at one of the long sides, tightly roll up each rectangle. Pinch the seam together, turn the loaf over, and tuck the ends under neatly. Place seam-side down in the prepared pans, cover, and let rise for about 30 minutes, or until doubled in bulk.

5. Place in a preheated 375°F oven and bake for 30 to 45 minutes, or until the loaves are very brown and hollow-sounding when rapped on the bottom with your knuckle. Cool on a wire rack before serving.

YIELD: 2 LARGE LOAVES

1 cup mashed potatoes, at room temperature (see TIP on page 63)

2 tablespoons (2 packets) active dry yeast

3 tablespoons honey

3 cups lukewarm water

1 cup nonfat dry milk powder

3 tablespoons oil

1 tablespoon plus 1 teaspoon salt

8–10 cups unbleached white flour

TIP When forming loaves for this (or any) recipe, if the dough fills the pans more than halfway, cut off a few small chunks. Form the chunks into rolls and bake them on a greased cake pan for about 20 to 25 minutes, or until they are brown and crusty.

CARAWAY POTATO BREAD

Unlike the Roadside Potato Bread (page 41), this caraway-studded loaf contains no oil and it has less milk, giving it a somewhat coarser texture. The recipe makes a particularly impressive loaf when baked in a large, round container, such as a 12-inch casserole, cake pan, or skillet with a bakeproof handle. (If you aren't sure about the handle, wrap it securely with aluminum foil.) For two smaller rounds, use 8-inch containers.

YIELD:
1 LARGE ROUND

1 cup mashed potatoes, at room temperature (see TIP on page 63)

2 tablespoons (2 packets) active dry yeast

1 tablespoon honey

3 cups lukewarm water

$\frac{1}{2}$ cup nonfat dry milk powder

$1\frac{1}{2}$ tablespoons salt

$1\frac{1}{2}$ tablespoons caraway seeds

8–10 cups unbleached white flour

1. Place the potatoes, yeast, honey, water, milk powder, salt, and caraway seeds in a dishpan or large bowl and stir with a wooden spoon. Add 4 cups of flour, and beat with the spoon until well blended.

2. Add 4 more cups of flour, then squeeze the mixture with your hands until the flour disappears. If it is too wet to pick up, add a little more flour. As soon as you can handle the dough, sprinkle with a bit more flour and begin to knead directly in the bowl (or on a floured board), adding more flour as necessary. Knead for about 8 minutes, or until the dough feels smooth and elastic. Shape into a ball.

3. Spread a little oil on the bottom and sides of the bowl. Add the ball of dough, then turn it over, oiled side up. Cover and set in a warm spot for about an hour, or until the dough doubles in bulk. Thoroughly grease (with oil or butter) a 12-inch round cake pan or casserole dish and set aside.

4. Punch down the risen dough, knead a minute to eliminate any air bubbles, and form into a ball. Place in the prepared pan, cover, and let rise for at least 40 minutes, or until doubled in bulk.

5. Cut a $\frac{1}{2}$-inch-deep cross on the top of the risen loaf, brush with cold water, and place in a preheated 400°F oven. Bake for about 45 minutes, or until the loaf is dark brown and hollow-sounding when rapped on the bottom with your knuckle. Cool on a wire rack before serving.

SEMOLINA BREAD

A particularly light and tender bread with a velvety texture, semolina (pane di semola) is especially popular in southern Italy's Puglia region, where semolina is a major crop. It requires a starter, which needs twelve to twenty-four hours to ferment, so you'll have to plan ahead and start this bread the day before you bake it. The recipe, which yields fairly small rounds, can be easily doubled.

1. To prepare the starter, stir the yeast and water in a medium-size bowl until the yeast is dissolved. Add the flour and stir until well mixed. Cover and let sit at room temperature for 12 to 24 hours.

2. To prepare the dough, place the yeast, water, oil, and salt in a dishpan or large bowl and stir with a wooden spoon. Add the starter, the white flour, and 1 cup of semolina, and beat with the spoon until well blended.

3. Add another $\frac{1}{2}$ cup semolina, then squeeze the mixture with your hands. If it is too wet to pick up, add a little more semolina. As soon as you can handle the dough (it will still be sticky), sprinkle with a light dusting of semolina and begin to knead directly in the bowl (or on a floured board), adding more semolina as necessary. Knead for 10 minutes, or until the dough feels smooth and elastic. Shape into a ball.

4. Spread a little olive oil on the bottom and sides of the bowl. Add the ball of dough, then turn it over, oiled side up. Cover and set in a warm spot for about an hour, or until the dough doubles in bulk. Lightly sprinkle a large baking sheet with semolina and set aside.

5. Punch down the risen dough, knead a minute to eliminate any air bubbles, and form into a ball. Cut in half, then shape each half into a round loaf. Place the loaves on the prepared baking sheet, leaving enough space between them to allow for expansion. Dust generously with semolina, and cut a $\frac{1}{2}$-inch-deep cross on top of each. Cover and let rise about 45 minutes, or until doubled in bulk.

6. Place in a preheated 400°F oven and bake for about 30 minutes, or until the loaves are golden brown and hollow-sounding when rapped on the bottom with your knuckle. Cool on a wire rack before serving.

**YIELD:
2 SMALL ROUNDS**

STARTER

1 teaspoon active dry yeast

$\frac{2}{3}$ cup lukewarm water

$\frac{3}{4}$ cup unbleached white flour

DOUGH

2 teaspoons active dry yeast

$\frac{3}{4}$ cup lukewarm water

2 tablespoons olive oil

1 tablespoon salt

1 cup unbleached white flour

$1\frac{1}{2}$–$1\frac{3}{4}$ cups semolina

CHALLAH

*The traditional Sabbath bread, challah (pronounced "holla") graces the tables of Jewish homes on Friday nights; it is also served on special occasions, including holidays, weddings, and bar or bat mitzvahs. Challah is a tender, light, and very beautiful bread; most commonly braided, it is sometimes made in a round to symbolize continuity or the cycle of life. This recipe makes one loaf. For large gatherings, it can be tripled (or even quadrupled) and formed into a giant round or a very large braided loaf that is **really** festive!*

YIELD:
1 MEDIUM LOAF

1 tablespoon (1 packet)
  active dry yeast

3/4 cup lukewarm water

1 tablespoon sugar

1 teaspoon salt

2 tablespoons oil

1 egg

Pinch saffron (optional),
  powdered and dissolved in
  1 teaspoon warm water*

2–3 cups unbleached
  white flour

1 egg yolk plus
  1 tablespoon water

2 tablespoons poppy seeds to
  sprinkle on loaf (optional)

*The addition of saffron heightens the yellow color of the bread.

1. Place the yeast, water, sugar, salt, oil, egg, saffron (if using), and 2 cups of flour in a large bowl and beat well with a wooden spoon. Add more flour a little at a time until you can handle the dough.

2. Sprinkle the dough with a little flour and begin to knead directly in the bowl (or on a floured board), adding more flour as necessary. Knead for 5 minutes, or until the dough is smooth and elastic. Shape into a ball.

3. Butter the bottom and sides of the bowl. Add the ball of dough, then turn it over, buttered side up. Cover and set in a warm spot for an hour, or until the dough doubles in bulk. Grease a large baking sheet and set aside.

4. Punch down the risen dough and cut into four equal pieces. Using your hands, roll three pieces into ropes about a foot long. Place them on the baking sheet and pinch together at one end. Then, working very carefully so as not to stretch the dough, loosely braid the strands. When you finish braiding, pinch the ends together, then neatly tuck both ends under the loaf.

5. Divide the remaining piece of dough into three pieces and form into a slender braid, about two-thirds the length of the large braid. Lay the small braid on top (along the center) of the big braid, and lightly brush the whole loaf with oil. Cover and let rise for an hour, or until doubled in bulk.

6. In a small bowl, beat together the egg yolk and cold water, then brush some on the top and sides of the loaf. Sprinkle with poppy seeds (if using), place in a preheated 375°F oven, and bake for 25 to 30 minutes, or until the loaf is a rich brown color and hollow-sounding when rapped on the bottom with your knuckle. Cool on a wire rack before serving.

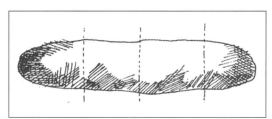

Divide the dough
into fourths.

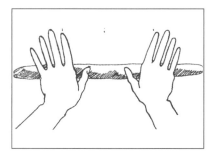

Roll out three pieces into
12 to 13-inch ropes.

Braid the three ropes.

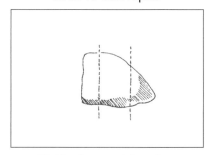

Divide the remaining piece
of dough into thirds.

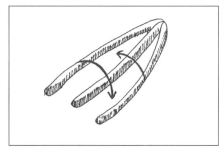

Roll the three pieces into
6 to 7-inch slender ropes, then braid.

Place the smaller braid on
top of the larger braid.

ROSEMARY-OLIVE OIL BREAD

Whether made with rosemary, sage, or no herbs at all, this olive oil bread is quite delicious.
And although you can use dried herbs in a pinch, fresh herbs are noticeably better.

YIELD:
1 MEDIUM ROUND

1 tablespoon (1 packet)
   active dry yeast

$\frac{1}{2}$ cup plus 2 teaspoons
   lukewarm water

$1\frac{1}{2}$–2 cups unbleached
   white flour

1 cup whole wheat flour

$\frac{1}{2}$ cup lukewarm water

1 tablespoon salt

1 tablespoon extra-virgin
   olive oil

1 tablespoon finely chopped
   fresh rosemary, or
   $1\frac{1}{2}$ teaspoons dried

1–2 tablespoons cornmeal
   for baking sheet

Sprig of rosemary to
   decorate the loaf

1. Place the yeast and $\frac{1}{2}$ cup plus 2 teaspoons warm water in a medium-sized bowl and stir with a wooden spoon until the yeast dissolves. Add $1\frac{1}{2}$ cups of white flour and stir to form a soft dough. Knead for 10 minutes, adding more flour as necessary. Shape into a ball.

2. Spread a little olive oil on the bottom and sides of the bowl. Add the ball of dough, then turn it over, oiled side up. Cover and set in a warm spot for about 45 minutes, or until the dough doubles in bulk.

3. Remove the dough from the bowl. Add $\frac{1}{2}$ cup white flour and $\frac{3}{4}$ cup whole wheat flour to the bowl. Place the dough on top, flatten it, and begin to knead. Add $\frac{1}{2}$ cup warm water, the salt, olive oil, and rosemary. Knead for 10 minutes, working in all of the ingredients, until the dough is smooth and elastic. Form into a ball.

4. Once again, oil the bowl and add the dough. Cover and set in a warm spot for 30 to 40 minutes, or until the dough doubles in bulk again. Lightly sprinkle a large baking sheet with cornmeal and set aside.

5. Punch down the risen dough, knead for a minute, then shape into a round loaf. Place the loaf on the prepared baking sheet and let rest for a minute or so. Cut two $\frac{1}{2}$-inch-deep parallel slashes across the top of the dough, then two more in the opposite direction (to form a tic-tac-toe design). Brush the loaf with cold water and top with a sprig of rosemary.

6. Place in a preheated 450°F oven. Toss a few ice cubes on the bottom of the oven (to create steam for a very crisp crust). Bake for 10 minutes, then toss in a couple more ice cubes. Continue baking for about 30 minutes, or until the loaf is browned and hollow-sounding when rapped on the bottom with your knuckle. Cool on a wire rack before serving.

4. Whole Grain Breads

These are the breads I love the most—the rich, hearty, crusty loaves crammed with grains and seeds, the kind you can almost live on. Maybe history has influenced my taste genes. After all, our earliest ancestors never even imagined white bread; the first breads were made from millet, barley, oats, rye, wheat, and other grains that had been coarsely crushed between stones. The rough dough was shaped into flat cakes then baked in hot ashes.

Today's whole grain breads have come a long way from their primitive beginning. Finely ground whole wheat, corn, rye, soy, triticale, millet, barley, and other grains are beautifully risen with yeast to make high, chewy-but-soft loaves. They are flavored with salt, sweeteners, oil, and spices; enhanced with seeds of flax, sesame, sunflower, pumpkin, poppy, and caraway, as well as olives, nuts, and fruit. The dough is then artfully shaped and baked in temperature-controlled ovens.

The variations are limited only by your imagination. Pumpernickel Bread gets its dark color and distinctive flavor from molasses and cocoa, Sprouted Wheat Bread owes it fascinating texture to sprouted wheat berries, the addition of oats gives Oatmeal Bread its special character, while Olive Bread owes its name to Calamata olives and good olive oil. Once you have mastered the art of making whole grain breads you can give your creativity free reign to develop your own combinations by adding your favorite seeds, spices, dried fruits, nuts, or cereals to any basic recipe, such as Honey Whole Wheat Bread.

Be aware that all whole grain breads make heavier doughs than white breads, so they are a little harder to knead. They tend to be stickier at first, too, because the dark flours contain less gluten than white. The dough will never become as satiny and shiny as white bread dough, but it will become bouncy and tractable with just a little bit of extra work. And that small extra effort is well worth the trouble because you will be able to turn out magnificent artisan loaves that are truly the staff of life.

If you need help when preparing the breads in this chapter, refer to the detailed steps for Basic Bread-Making in Chapter 2, beginning on page 18.

HONEY WHOLE WHEAT BREAD

As whole grain breads go, this one is among the simplest, with but a single grain—whole wheat. It is, however, a hearty bread with a chewy texture and good flavor. It keeps well and makes excellent toast and sandwiches. Keep in mind that because whole wheat flour contains less gluten than white flour, the kneaded dough will not be quite as smooth as dough made purely from white flour.

YIELD:
2 LARGE LOAVES

2 tablespoons (2 packets)
    active dry yeast

2½ cups lukewarm water

4 tablespoons honey

4 tablespoons oil

1 tablespoon salt

8–10 cups whole wheat flour

1. Place the yeast, water, honey, oil, and salt in a dishpan or large bowl, and stir with a wooden spoon. Add 6 cups of flour and beat with the spoon for a minute or two, or until well blended.

2. Add 2 more cups of flour, then squeeze the mixture with your hands until the flour disappears. If it is too wet to pick up, add a little more flour. As soon as you can handle the dough, sprinkle with a bit more flour and begin to knead directly in the bowl (or on a floured board), adding more flour as necessary. Knead for 10 minutes, or until the dough is fairly smooth and elastic. Shape into a ball.

3. Spread a little oil on the bottom and sides of the bowl. Add the ball of dough, then turn it over, oiled side up. Cover and set in a warm spot for about an hour, or until the dough doubles in bulk. Thoroughly grease (with oil or butter) two 9-x-5-inch bread pans and set aside.

4. Punch down the risen dough and form into a ball. Cut in half, and pat each half into a flattened rectangle that is a little longer than the pans. Starting at one of the long sides, tightly roll up each rectangle. Pinch the seam together, turn the loaf over, and tuck the ends under neatly. Place the loaves seam-side down in the prepared pans, cover, and let rise about 30 to 40 minutes, or until doubled in bulk.

5. Cut a ½-inch-deep slash lengthwise down the center of each risen loaf. Place in a preheated 375°F oven and bake for about 40 minutes, or until the loaves are very brown and hollow-sounding when rapped on the bottom with your knuckle. Cool on a wire rack before serving.

VARIATIONS

Rich Honey Whole Wheat Bread For a richer, "cakier" version of this bread, add 1 egg to ingredients in Step 1.

Light Whole Wheat Bread Use half whole wheat flour, and half unbleached white. (It doesn't have to be exactly half and half.)

Bran Bread Add 1 cup bran (miller's bran, not bran cereal) after beating the dough in Step 1.

Raisin Bran Bread Add 1 cup bran (miller's bran, not bran cereal) and 1 cup raisins after beating the dough in Step 1. For a sweeter version, add 3 additional tablespoons honey and 1 teaspoon cinnamon.

75-MINUTE HEALTH BREAD

This recipe is loosely based on one developed by a Danish scientist during World War II. It is very rich in protein and low in fat, and can be prepared (start to finish) in an hour and a quarter. "Can be," however, doesn't necessarily mean it "will be." If you are an inexperienced baker, it might take an hour and a half—still pretty fast for a kneaded yeast bread.

YIELD: 2 LARGE LOAVES

3 tablespoons (3 packets) active dry yeast

$\frac{1}{2}$ cup lukewarm water

1 or 2 drops honey

1$\frac{1}{3}$ cups nonfat dry milk powder

2 cups lukewarm water

1 tablespoon honey

1 tablespoon salt

1 cup wheat germ

2 cups whole wheat flour

3–4 cups unbleached white flour

TIP To activate the yeast as quickly as possible, warm the mixing bowl first. Simply rinse the bowl with hot water, dry it, then immediately begin preparing the yeast mixture.

1. Place the yeast, $\frac{1}{2}$ cup lukewarm water, and a drop or two of honey in a dishpan or large bowl and stir with a wooden spoon until the yeast dissolves. Add the milk powder, 2 cups of lukewarm water, honey, salt, wheat germ, and whole wheat flour. Beat for 2 minutes with the spoon.

2. Add 3 cups of white flour and continue to mix until it becomes too stiff to mix with the spoon. Sprinkle with flour and begin to knead directly in the bowl (or on a floured board), adding more flour, a little at a time, as necessary. Knead for about 10 minutes, or until the dough is soft and elastic, but still somewhat sticky. Shape into a ball.

3. Thoroughly grease (with oil or butter) two 9-x-5-inch bread pans and set aside. Cut the ball of dough in half, and form each half into a loaf. (If the dough is too sticky to form neat loaves, wet your hands with cold water and smooth the tops of the loaves.) Place the loaves in the prepared pans. Cut a $\frac{1}{2}$-inch-deep slash lengthwise down the center of each loaf.

4. Place the pans in a cold oven, then turn the temperature to 150°F. Let the loaves sit in the oven for 15 minutes (it's a good idea to set your timer for this), or until the dough doubles in bulk. Then increase the heat to 350°F, and continue baking for about 50 minutes, or until the loaves are well browned and hollow-sounding when rapped on the bottom with your knuckle. Cool on a wire rack before serving.

PEASANT BREAD

It would be hard to say just what kind of peasant made this bread first, but it is typical of many of the country breads of Europe, especially in the middle and eastern sectors. It has a hard, crunchy crust and a hearty dark-colored crumb.

1. Place the yeast, water, coffee, cornmeal, salt, and 9 cups of flour in a dishpan or large bowl. Stir with a wooden spoon until the mixture starts to leave the sides of the bowl. Let rest for 10 minutes.

2. Sprinkle 1 cup of flour over the dough and on your hands and begin to knead directly in the bowl (or on a floured board), adding more flour as necessary. Knead for 10 minutes, or until the dough is fairly smooth and elastic. Shape into a ball.

3. Spread a little oil on the bottom and sides of the bowl. Add the ball of dough, then turn it over, oiled side up. Cover the bowl with a clean dish-towel that has been wrung out in cold water, and set in a warm spot for about an hour, or until the dough doubles in bulk. Punch down the risen dough, form into a ball, and let rise a second time for 40 minutes, or until doubled in bulk. Sprinkle cornmeal on a large baking sheet and set aside.

4. Punch down the risen dough and form into a ball. Cut in half, then shape each half into a round loaf. Place the loaves on the prepared baking sheet. Brush the tops with cold water, and let rise for 20 minutes.

5. Brush the tops with cold water again, cut a $\frac{1}{2}$-inch-deep large cross on top of each loaf and place in a preheated 375°F oven. Bake for about 1 hour, or until the loaves are dark brown and hollow-sounding when rapped on the bottom with your knuckle. Cool on a wire rack before serving.

YIELD: 2 LARGE ROUNDS

2 tablespoons (2 packets) active dry yeast

2 cups lukewarm water

2½ cups lukewarm coffee (brewed or instant)

½ cup yellow cornmeal

2 tablespoons salt

10–11 cups whole wheat flour

1–2 tablespoons cornmeal for the baking sheet

TIP Begin kneading very sticky dough with your fist (instead of your palm), taking care to scrape the bottom and sides of the bowl often. Continue kneading this way until the dough begins to take shape. A sprinkle of flour on the dough and on your hands is also helpful.

WHEAT-BERRY BREAD

This is another hearty, wholesome bread with a delicious, nut-like flavor.
You can buy wheat berries in any health food store or in any market that sells whole grains.
Few people will be able to identify them in the bread.

YIELD: 2 LARGE ROUNDS

1 cup water

½ cup wheat berries

1 cup cold water

2 cups lukewarm water

3 tablespoons (3 packets) active dry yeast

½ cup honey

½ cup oil

1 tablespoon salt

8 cups whole wheat flour

2–4 cups unbleached white flour

1–2 tablespoons cornmeal for the baking sheet

TIP For an extra-crisp crust, brush or spray the loaves with cold water several times during baking.

1. Bring 1 cup of water to a boil in a small saucepan, then add the wheat berries. Reduce the heat to low, cover, and simmer for about 20 minutes, or until all of the water is absorbed. Add the cold water to the cooked berries, then transfer the mixture (be sure it's no more than lukewarm) to a dishpan or large bowl. Add the lukewarm water, yeast, honey, oil, and salt and stir with a wooden spoon. Add the whole wheat flour and continue stirring for 1 or 2 minutes, or until well blended.

2. Add 1 cup of white flour, then squeeze the mixture with your hands until the flour disappears. If it is too wet to pick up, add a little more flour. As soon as you can handle the dough, sprinkle with a bit more flour and begin to knead directly in the bowl (or on a floured board), adding more flour as necessary. Knead for 7 or 8 minutes, or until the dough is elastic and easy to handle. Shape into a ball.

3. Spread a little oil on the bottom and sides of the bowl. Add the ball of dough, then turn it over, oiled side up. Cover and set in a warm spot for about an hour, or until the dough doubles in bulk. Sprinkle some cornmeal on a large baking sheet and set aside.

4. Punch down the risen dough, knead for a minute to eliminate any large air bubbles that cling to the berries, and form into a ball. Cut in half, then shape each half into a round. Place the loaves on the prepared baking sheet, leaving enough space between them to allow for expansion.

5. Cut a ½-inch-deep cross on top of each loaf. Place in a cold oven, then turn the temperature to 350°F. Bake for about 1 hour, or until the loaves are browned and hollow-sounding when rapped on the bottom with your knuckle. Cool on a wire rack before serving.

CORN-WHEAT BREAD

This unusually dense, moist loaf keeps well and is good to enjoy any time; but I find it a particularly satisfying breakfast bread that's guaranteed to stick to your ribs all morning. Try it toasted.

1. Put 1 cup of cold water into a small saucepan, then stir in the cornmeal. Stirring *constantly* (to prevent lumps), bring the mixture to a boil. Reduce the heat to low and simmer (still stirring) for 2 to 3 minutes, or until the cornmeal is very thick. Transfer the mixture to a dishpan or large bowl and add the cold water. Stir with a wooden spoon until the mixture has cooled to lukewarm.

2. Add the yeast, milk powder, brown sugar, salt, and 3 cups of flour to the cooled cornmeal. Beat with a wooden spoon for 1 or 2 minutes, or until the mixture is well blended and free of cornmeal lumps.

3. Add 2 more cups of flour, then squeeze the mixture with your hands until the flour disappears. If it is too wet to pick up, add a little more flour, but be aware that this tends to be a sticky dough that is never really easy to handle (don't be put off by it, it's all that cornmeal mush that does it—and it's worth the trouble). Begin to knead directly in the bowl (or on a floured board), adding more flour as necessary. Knead for 6 or 7 minutes, then shape the dough into a ball.

4. Spread a little oil on the bottom and sides of the bowl. Add the ball of dough, then turn it over, oiled side up. Cover and set in a warm spot for about an hour, or until the dough doubles in bulk. Thoroughly grease (with oil or butter) two 9-x-5-inch bread pans and set aside.

5. Punch down the risen dough, knead for a minute (the dough will be much more manageable at this point), and shape into a ball. Cut in half, and pat each half into a flattened rectangle that is a little longer than the pans. Starting at one of the long sides, tightly roll up each rectangle. Pinch the seam together, turn the loaf over, and tuck the ends under neatly. Place seam-side down in the prepared pans, cover, and let rise for 45 minutes, or until doubled in bulk (the loaves will just about reach the tops of the pans).

6. Place in a preheated 375°F oven and bake for about 45 minutes, or until the loaves are very brown and hollow-sounding when rapped on the bottom with your knuckle. Cool on a wire rack before serving.

YIELD: 2 LARGE LOAVES

1 cup water

½ cup yellow cornmeal

1½ cups cold water

2 tablespoons (2 packets) active dry yeast

⅓ cup nonfat dry milk powder

3 tablespoons brown sugar

1 tablespoon salt

5–6 cups whole wheat flour

OATMEAL BREAD

This dark oatmeal bread is chewy and slightly sweet. It goes well with jam for breakfast or teatime and makes excellent toast. It also keeps well. This is a good bread to bake in 1-pound metal coffee cans (just don't forget to grease them well and sprinkle with cornmeal before adding the dough). If you prefer loaves with less sweetness, cut the amount of molasses in half.

YIELD:
2 MEDIUM LOAVES

1 ½ cups oats (not instant)

2 cups boiling water

1 tablespoon (1 packet) active dry yeast

½ cup lukewarm water

½ cup molasses

¼ cup oil

1 tablespoon salt

2 cups unbleached white flour

2–3 cups whole wheat flour

1. Place the oats in a dishpan or large bowl and cover with the boiling water. Stir and set aside. Mix the yeast with the lukewarm water. When the oat mixture has cooled to lukewarm, add the yeast mixture, molasses, oil, salt, and white flour. Beat well with a wooden spoon for 1 to 2 minutes.

2. Add 2 cups of whole wheat flour, then squeeze the mixture with your hands until the flour disappears. If it is too wet to pick up, add a little more flour. As soon as you can handle the dough, sprinkle with a bit more flour and begin to knead directly in the bowl (or on a floured board), adding more flour as necessary. Knead for about 5 minutes, or until the dough feels springy. Shape into a ball.

3. Spread a little oil on the bottom and sides of the bowl. Add the ball of dough, then turn it over, oiled side up. Cover and set in a warm spot for about an hour, or until the dough doubles in bulk. Thoroughly grease (with oil or butter) two 8-x-4-inch bread pans and set aside.

4. Punch down the risen dough and shape into a ball. Cut in half, and pat each half into a flattened rectangle that is a little longer than the pans. Starting at one of the long sides, tightly roll up each rectangle. Pinch the seam together, turn the loaf over, and tuck the ends under neatly. Place seam-side down in the prepared pans, cover, and let rise for about 45 minutes, or until doubled in bulk (the loaves will just about reach the top of the pans).

5. Place in a preheated 350°F oven and bake for about 50 minutes, or until the loaves are browned and hollow-sounding when rapped on the bottom with your knuckle. Cool on a wire rack before serving.

VARIATIONS

Light Oatmeal Bread Use all unbleached white flour, and substitute honey for the molasses.

Oatmeal Fruit-Nut Bread After the first rising, work $\frac{1}{2}$ cup chopped walnuts or pecans, and 1 cup chopped prunes, dates, or dried apricots into the dough.

ANADAMA BREAD

An old legend traces this cornmeal bread to a New England fisherman, whose wife, Anna, gave him cornmeal mush for breakfast day in and day out. Our fisherman grumbled and complained, until one day, just before Anna tossed the cornmeal into the pot of boiling water, he snatched it from her hand and dumped it into a bowl. Then, furiously grabbing what was available, he threw in some molasses, flour, and so forth, and proceeded to make what turned out to be a delicious bread. All the time he was kneading the dough, he kept muttering, "Anna, damn her!"

1. Place the yeast, water, molasses, oil, salt, and cornmeal in a dishpan or large bowl and stir with a wooden spoon. Add the white flour, and beat with the spoon until well blended.

2. Add 2 cups of whole wheat flour, then squeeze the mixture with your hands until the flour disappears. If it is too wet to pick up, add a little more flour. As soon as you can handle the dough, sprinkle with a bit more flour and begin to knead directly in the bowl (or on a floured board), adding more flour as necessary. Knead about 5 minutes, or until the dough is elastic and resistant. (It will be somewhat grainy because of the cornmeal.) Shape into a ball.

3. Spread a little oil on the bottom and sides of the bowl. Add the ball of dough, then turn it over, oiled side up. Cover and set in a warm spot for about an hour, or until the dough doubles in bulk. Thoroughly grease (with oil or butter) two 8-x-4-inch bread pans and set aside.

YIELD:
2 MEDIUM LOAVES

1 tablespoon (1 packet) active dry yeast

$1\frac{1}{2}$ cups lukewarm water

$\frac{1}{4}$ cup molasses

2 tablespoons oil

1 tablespoon salt

$\frac{1}{2}$ cup yellow cornmeal

2 cups unbleached white flour

2–3 cups whole wheat flour

4. Punch down the risen dough, knead for a minute or so, and form into a ball. Cut in half, and pat each half into a flattened rectangle that is a little longer than the pans. Starting at one of the long sides, tightly roll up each rectangle. Pinch the seam together, turn the loaf over, and tuck the ends under neatly. Place seam-side down in the prepared pans.

5. Place the pans in a preheated 425°F oven for 10 minutes, then turn down the heat to 350°F. Bake for about 35 minutes more, or until the loaves are browned and hollow-sounding when rapped on the bottom with your knuckle. Cool on a wire rack before serving.

Grow Your Own Sprouts

1. Place about 4 tablespoons of wheat berries (or kernels) into a colander, and rinse them under cold running water. Set the colander in a large bowl (to catch the water drops), and cover with a clean kitchen towel. Place in a warm out-of-the-way corner of the kitchen.

2. Every day, water the berries three or four times (after meals and at bedtime is an easy routine to remember). Simply hold the colander under running water for a few seconds to rinse the berries, then return it to the emptied bowl. Keep the berries warm and dark under the towel.

3. By the end of the third day, the berries will be well sprouted and ready to use.

As the berries sprout, much of their wheat starch is converted to sugar. Take a taste. You'll be surprised by their sweetness. If you have more sprouts than you need for a recipe, such as the Sprouted Wheat Bread on the next page, keep them in a plastic bag in the refrigerator, where they will keep for several days. Munch on them as snacks, toss them into salads and omelets, or add them to sandwiches.

You can use the same method for sprouting many kinds of seeds and beans—sesame and sunflower seeds, lentils, soybeans, alfalfa, and chickpeas. Sprouted mung beans are commonly used in Chinese-style dishes; they are also great additions to egg, meat, and seafood dishes, as well as breads.

SPROUTED WHEAT BREAD

Sprouts give this delicious vitamin-rich bread a most unusual flavor and fascinating texture (it looks as if it needs a shave). Although you can buy wheat sprouts, it's more fun (and very easy) to grow your own. The inset on the previous page shows you how.

1. Place the yeast, water, honey, salt, sprouts and white flour in a dishpan or large bowl and beat with a wooden spoon for 2 minutes. Add 2 cups of the whole wheat flour, and continue to beat, adding more flour, a little at a time, until the dough is too stiff to beat.

2. Add 1 more cup of whole wheat flour, then squeeze the mixture with your hands until the flour disappears. If it is too wet to pick up, add a little more flour. As soon as you can handle the dough, sprinkle with a bit more flour and begin to knead directly in the bowl (or on a floured board). Knead for about 10 minutes, or until the dough is easy to handle and feels springy, although somewhat sticky. Shape into a ball.

3. Spread a little oil on the bottom and sides of the bowl. Add the ball of dough, then turn it over, oiled side up. Cover and set in a warm spot for about an hour, or until the dough doubles in bulk. Thoroughly grease (with oil or butter) two 9-x-5-inch bread pans and set aside.

4. Punch down the risen dough, knead for a minute or so, and form into a ball. Cut in half, and pat each half into a flattened rectangle that is a little longer than the pans. Starting at one of the long sides, tightly roll up each rectangle. Pinch the seam together, turn the loaf over, and tuck the ends under neatly. Place seam-side down in the prepared pans, cover, and let rise about 30 minutes, or until the dough doubles in bulk.

5. Place the pans in a preheated 350°F oven and bake for about 1 hour, or until the loaves are very brown and hollow-sounding when rapped on the bottom with your knuckle. Cool on a wire rack before serving.

YIELD: 2 LARGE LOAVES

2 tablespoons (2 packets) active dry yeast

3 cups lukewarm water

3 tablespoons honey

1 tablespoon salt

2 cups wheat sprouts (see inset on page 56)

3½ cups unbleached white flour

4–5 cups whole wheat flour

WHEATENA WHEAT BREAD

A finely cracked wheat that is often enjoyed as a hot breakfast cereal,
Wheatena provides an irresistible nutty crunch to this nutritious bread.
Try a couple slices for breakfast instead of a bowl of cereal.

YIELD: 2 LARGE LOAVES

3 cups lukewarm water

2 tablespoons (2 packets) active dry yeast

$2/3$ cup nonfat dry milk powder

1 cup uncooked Wheatena

2 tablespoons honey

2 tablespoons oil

1 tablespoon salt

6–8 cups whole wheat flour

1. Place all of the ingredients except the flour in a dishpan or large bowl and stir with a wooden spoon. Add 3 cups of flour and beat with the spoon until well blended.

2. Add 3 more cups of flour, then squeeze the mixture with your hands until the flour disappears. If it is too wet to pick up, add a little more flour. As soon as you can handle the dough, sprinkle with a bit more flour and begin to knead directly in the bowl (or on a floured surface), adding more flour as necessary. Knead for 8 to 10 minutes, or until the dough is very elastic. Shape into a ball.

3. Spread a little oil on the bottom and sides of the bowl. Add the ball of dough, then turn it over, oiled side up. Cover and set in a warm spot for about an hour, or until the dough doubles in bulk. Thoroughly grease (with oil or butter) two 9-x-5-inch bread pans and set aside.

4. Punch down the risen dough, knead for a minute, and form into a ball. Cut in half, and pat each half into a flattened rectangle that is a little longer than the pans. Starting at one of the long sides, tightly roll up each rectangle. Pinch the seam together, turn the loaf over, and tuck the ends under neatly. Place seam-side down in the prepared pans, cover, and let rise about 30 to 40 minutes, or until the dough doubles in bulk.

5. Cut a $1/2$-inch-deep slash lengthwise down the center of each loaf. Brush the tops with cold water, and place in a preheated 400°F oven. Bake for about 40 minutes, or until the loaves are very brown and hollow-sounding when rapped on the bottom with your knuckle. Cool on a wire rack before serving.

SOY BREAD

Milled from soybeans, soy flour is one of our richest vegetable sources of protein. Even a small amount of soy flour adds greatly to the nutritional value of any bread—and this bread almost qualifies as a meal in itself. It also happens to have a distinctive and magnificent flavor. Because soy flour is lacking in gluten, it makes a sticky dough, which is worked in a rather unconventional manner.

1. Place the yeast, water, milk powder, oil, honey, and salt in a dishpan or large bowl and stir with a wooden spoon. Add the white flour and soy flour and continue to stir. Add 4 cups of whole wheat flour and mix with the spoon until well blended.

2. Sprinkle a little flour on top of the dough, which will be very sticky, and knead it just long enough to mix thoroughly (you won't be able to do much more than that). Shape it into a very soft, sticky ball.

3. Spread a little oil on the bottom and sides of another large bowl. Add the ball of dough, then turn it over, oiled side up. Cover and set in a warm spot for about 45 minutes, or until the dough doubles in bulk. Thoroughly grease (with oil or butter) two 8-x-4-inch bread pans, and sprinkle the bottoms with a little cornmeal. Set aside.

4. Punch down the risen dough (it will be much more manageable at this point). Add enough flour to make it easy to knead, then knead for 5 to 10 minutes, or until the dough feels smooth and elastic. Shape into a ball.

5. Cut the ball of dough in half, then pat each half into a flattened rectangle that is a little longer than the pans. Starting at one of the long sides, tightly roll up each rectangle. Pinch the seam together, turn the loaf over, and tuck the ends under neatly. Place seam-side down in the prepared pans, cover, and let rise for about 30 minutes, or until doubled in bulk.

6. Place in a preheated 375°F oven and bake for 35 to 40 minutes, or until the loaves are very brown and hollow-sounding when rapped on the bottom with your knuckle. Cool on a wire rack before serving.

YIELD: 2 MEDIUM LOAVES

- 2 tablespoons (2 packets) active dry yeast
- 2½ cups lukewarm water
- ⅔ cup nonfat dry milk powder
- ¼ cup oil
- ½ cup honey
- 1½ tablespoons salt
- 1 cup unbleached white flour
- 1⅓ cups soy flour
- 4–5 cups whole wheat flour
- 1–2 tablespoons cornmeal for pans

NORWEGIAN RYE BREAD

Rye flour is somewhat hard to work because it makes a very sticky dough,
but rye bread fanciers will find the extra effort worthwhile. This recipe produces
a fine-grained bread that is smooth and light in color. Cardamom gives it an interesting,
slightly exotic taste. Try a slice topped with cream cheese and your favorite jam.

YIELD:
2 MEDIUM ROUNDS

2 tablespoons (2 packets)
   active dry yeast

$2\frac{1}{2}$ cups lukewarm water

2 tablespoons sugar

$\frac{2}{3}$ cup nonfat dry milk powder

4 tablespoons oil

1 cup wheat germ

1 tablespoon salt

Scant teaspoon powdered
   cardamom

$3\frac{1}{2}$ cups unbleached
   white flour

2–3 cups rye flour

1 egg white plus
   1 tablespoon cold water

1–2 tablespoons cornmeal
   for pans

1. Place the yeast, water, sugar, milk powder, oil, wheat germ, salt, and cardamom in a dishpan or large bowl and stir with a wooden spoon. Add the white flour and beat with the spoon for 3 minutes.

2. Add 2 cups of rye flour, then squeeze the mixture with your hands until the flour disappears. If it is too wet to pick up, add a little more flour. As soon as you can handle the dough, sprinkle with a bit more flour and begin to knead directly in the bowl (or on a floured board), adding flour as necessary. Knead for about 5 minutes, or until the dough is smooth and elastic. Shape into a ball.

3. Spread a little oil on the bottom and sides of the bowl. Add the ball of dough, then turn it over, oiled side up. Cover and set in a warm spot for about an hour, or until the dough doubles in bulk. Thoroughly grease (with oil or butter) two 8-inch round cake pans or pie tins and set aside.

4. Punch down the risen dough and form into a ball. Cut in half, and shape each half into a round that is higher in the center than on the sides (do this by placing the palms of your hands on opposite sides of the dough and slapping it down on the counter while turning repeatedly). Place in the prepared pans. Leave the tops as they are for a rugged look, or smooth them with a little cold water. Cover the loaves and let rise about 30 minutes, or until doubled in bulk.

5. Cut a $\frac{1}{2}$-inch-deep cross on the top of each risen loaf (or 5 or 6 short slashes in a circle, like flower petals). In a small bowl, beat together the egg white and cold water; using a pastry brush or your fingers, brush some on each loaf. Place in a preheated 400°F oven and bake for 30 to 35 minutes, or until the loaves are browned and hollow-sounding when rapped on the bottom with your knuckle. Cool on a wire rack before serving.

POTATO-RYE BREAD

Here is a light, tender rye with the fine texture that is characteristic of potato bread. The potatoes add moistness, so this bread keeps especially well.

1. Place the yeast, water, potatoes, molasses, salt, and caraway seeds in a dishpan or large bowl and stir with a wooden spoon. Add the rye flour and beat with the spoon until well blended.

2. Add 2 cups of white flour (and as much more as is necessary to make a soft dough). Squeeze the mixture with your hands until the flour disappears. If it is too wet to pick up, add a little more flour. As soon as you can handle the dough, sprinkle it and your hands with a bit more flour and begin to knead directly in the bowl (or on a floured board), adding more flour as necessary (the dough will be soft and sticky). Knead for 5 to 7 minutes, or until the dough feels fairly smooth and elastic. Shape into a ball.

3. Spread a little oil on the bottom and sides of the bowl. Add the ball of dough, then turn it over, oiled side up. Cover and set in a warm spot for about an hour, or until the dough doubles in bulk. Thoroughly grease (with oil or butter) a 12-inch round cake pan or casserole dish, sprinkle the bottom and sides with cornmeal and set aside.

4. Punch down the risen dough, knead for 2 to 3 minutes, and form into a round loaf. Place in the prepared pan, cover, and let rise about 30 minutes, or until doubled in bulk.

5. Cut a $\frac{1}{2}$-inch deep cross on top of the risen loaf. In a small bowl, beat together the egg white and cold water; using a pastry brush or your fingers, brush some on each loaf. Place in a preheated 375°F oven and bake for about 40 minutes, or until the loaf is dark brown and hollow-sounding when rapped on the bottom with your knuckle. Cool on a wire rack before serving.

YIELD:
1 LARGE ROUND

1 tablespoon (1 packet) active dry yeast

$1\frac{1}{4}$ cups lukewarm water

1 cup mashed potatoes, at room temperature (see TIP on page 63)

4 tablespoons molasses

1 tablespoon salt

1 tablespoon caraway seeds

$1\frac{1}{2}$ cups rye flour

2–3 cups unbleached white flour

1 egg white plus 1 tablespoon cold water

1–2 tablespoons cornmeal for pan

FYI A round loaf of bread is also known as a *boule*— the French word for "ball."

RYE-CORN-POTATO BREAD

This bread is hearty, dense, and absolutely delicious! Since the dough is heavy and hard to handle,
you'll need to use a very large bowl to prepare it. A plastic dishpan is perfect; however, if you
don't have one, be sure to use your largest container—a roasting pan is a good choice.

YIELD: 2 VERY LARGE ROUNDS

1 cup yellow cornmeal

1½ cups cold water

1½ cups boiling water

1 tablespoon (1 packet) active dry yeast

¼ cup lukewarm water

2 cups mashed potatoes, at room temperature (see TIP on page 63)

2 tablespoons salt

2 tablespoons oil

1 tablespoon caraway seeds

1 tablespoon sugar

2 cups unbleached white flour

4–6 cups rye flour

1 egg white plus 1 tablespoon cold water

1–2 tablespoons cornmeal for baking sheet

1. Mix the cornmeal and cold water in a saucepan. Add the boiling water and place on the stove over high heat. Bring to a boil, then simmer for 2 minutes, stirring constantly (to avoid lumps). Set aside to cool.

2. Place the yeast and lukewarm water in a dishpan or very large mixing bowl. Stir with a wooden spoon, then add the potatoes and cooked cornmeal (both cooled to lukewarm), salt, oil, caraway seeds, sugar, and white flour. Beat with the spoon until well blended.

3. Add 3 cups of rye flour and stir it into the mixture. Add more flour, a little at a time, until you can't stir anymore. Then squeeze the mixture with your hands until the flour disappears; if it is too wet to pick up, add a little more flour. As soon as you can handle the dough, sprinkle with a bit more flour and begin to knead directly in the bowl (or on a floured board), adding more flour as necessary. The dough will be very heavy, sticky, and hard to handle, but don't give up—as you knead it will get easier. This dough will never be as smooth and elastic as most, but knead it for at least 10 minutes. Shape into a ball.

4. Spread a little oil on the bottom and sides of the bowl. Add the ball of dough, then turn it over, oiled side up. Cover and set in a warm spot for an hour or more, or until the dough doubles in bulk. Lightly sprinkle a large baking sheet with cornmeal and set aside.

5. Punch down the risen dough and form into a ball. Cut in half, then shape each half into a round loaf. (Slap the rounds down hard on the counter a few times as you form them.) Place the loaves on the prepared baking sheet, leaving enough space between them to allow for expansion. Cover, and let rise about 40 minutes, or until not quite doubled in bulk.

6. Cut a $\frac{1}{2}$-inch-deep tic-tac-toe on top of each risen loaf. In a small bowl, beat together the egg white and cold water, then brush some on each loaf. Place in a preheated 350°F oven. Bake for 30 minutes, brush again with the egg glaze, and continue to bake 30 minutes more, or until the loaves are dark brown and hollow-sounding when rapped on the bottom with your knuckle. Cool on a wire rack before serving.

TIP When a bread recipe calls for "mashed potatoes," some bakers use only potatoes that have been freshly boiled and mashed—and they add the cooled cooking liquid (instead of plain water) to the dough. If, however, you don't have the time (or desire) to make the real thing, instant mashed potatoes can serve as a fine substitute. When using instant varieties, simply check the package directions for the amount of powder (or flakes) necessary to make the required amount needed in the recipe. You will be mixing this with lukewarm water only—no milk, butter, or seasonings called for on the package.

Let's say, for instance, the recipe calls for 1 cup of mashed potatoes. You would mix the dried potatoes with the requisite amount of lukewarm water according to the package instructions, plus extra lukewarm water to make up for the omitted milk. This will come to approximately 1 cup. Stir the mixture, let sit a minute to thicken, and use.

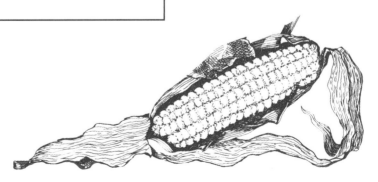

PUMPERNICKEL BREAD

It is said that this bread takes its name from the fifteenth-century German baker, Nicholas Pumper. We can't vouch for Herr Pumper, but we are certain that this bread is one of the great German specialties. It is particularly good served with cold cuts or cheese—with plenty of mustard, of course—and a pickle on the side. A word of advice: the dough for this bread is an uncommonly hard one to knead, so plan to make it on a day when you are feeling strong and energetic.

YIELD: 2 LARGE LOAVES

3 tablespoons (3 packets) active dry yeast

1½ cups lukewarm water

4 tablespoons dark molasses

4 tablespoons unsweetened cocoa

2 tablespoons oil

1½ tablespoons caraway seeds

1½ tablespoons salt

2¾ cups rye flour

2–3 cups unbleached white flour

1–2 tablespoons cornmeal for the baking sheet

1. Place the yeast and water in a dishpan or large bowl. Stir with a wooden spoon, then add the molasses, cocoa, oil, caraway seeds, salt, and rye flour. Beat with the spoon for 2 minutes.

2. Add 2 cups of white flour, then squeeze the mixture with your hands until the flour disappears. If it is too wet to pick up, add a little more flour. As soon as the dough is just stiff enough to knead, cover and let it rest for 10 minutes. Begin kneading the dough, but be aware that it will be very hard to do. Knead for 10 minutes, or until the dough feels smooth (and you are probably exhausted). Shape into a ball.

3. Spread a little oil on the bottom and sides of the bowl. Add the ball of dough, then turn it over, oiled side up. Cover and set in a warm spot for at least an hour, or until the dough doubles in bulk. Lightly sprinkle a large baking sheet with cornmeal and set aside.

4. Punch down the risen dough, cover, and let rise again for about 40 minutes. After the second rising, punch down the dough, knead for a minute or so, and form into a ball. Cut in half, then shape each half into an oval-shaped loaf (like a fat submarine). Spread a few drops of cold water on top of each loaf (to act as glue) and sprinkle with caraway seeds. Place the loaves on the prepared baking sheet, leaving enough space between them to allow for expansion. Cover and let rise for about 1 hour.

5. Cut two or more ½-inch-deep slashes across the top of each risen loaf. Place in a preheated 375°F oven and bake for 30 to 35 minutes, or until the loaves are dark, dark brown and hollow-sounding when rapped on the bottom with your knuckle. Cool on a wire rack before serving. As an option, while the bread is still warm, polish the top with a small lump of butter held in a piece of paper towel. This will give the loaf its characteristic shiny finish.

VARIATION

Light Pumpernickel Bread Reduce the rye flour to 2 cups and use an additional $^3/_4$ cup unbleached white flour. Also leave out the cocoa, and use honey instead of molasses.

WHEAT GERM BATTER BREAD

This nutritious no-knead bread is quick and easy to make—and absolutely delicious. Like all yeast batter breads, the dough will be very sticky, so be sure to generously grease the pans (even nonstick types) and sprinkle them well with cornmeal.

1. Generously grease (with butter or oil) two 8-x-4-inch bread pans, sprinkle well with cornmeal and set aside.

2. Place all of the ingredients in a large mixing bowl and beat well for 10 minutes with a wooden spoon, or use an electric mixer with a dough hook. (You are not going to knead this dough, so the beating and the rising are the only workouts it will get). Cover and set in a warm spot for about 45 minutes, or until the batter almost doubles in bulk.

3. Poke down the risen batter with your fingers, divide it in half with a knife, and put each half into the prepared pans. Cover and let rise about 30 to 35 minutes, or until the dough almost doubles in bulk.

4. Place the pans in a preheated 375°F oven and bake for about 45 minutes, or until the loaves are dark brown and hollow-sounding when rapped on the bottom with your knuckle. Cool on a wire rack before serving.

YIELD:
2 MEDIUM LOAVES

2 tablespoons (2 packets) active dry yeast

2 cups lukewarm water

$^1/_3$ cup nonfat dry milk powder

2 tablespoons honey

2 tablespoons oil

2 teaspoons salt

3 cups whole wheat flour

1 cup wheat germ

2–3 tablespoons cornmeal for pans

WHOLE WHEAT BATTER BREAD

The flavor of this no-knead whole wheat bread is as good as the conventional, but it has a much coarser texture and doesn't keep as well. Unless you plan to use both loaves promptly, wrap one as soon as it has cooled completely, and freeze it. Because the dough is soft and sticky, be sure to grease the pans generously (even nonstick types), and sprinkle them well with cornmeal. If you don't, the bread won't leave the pans without a struggle!

YIELD:
2 LARGE LOAVES

3 tablespoons (3 packets) active dry yeast

4 cups lukewarm water

4 tablespoons honey

1 1/2 tablespoons salt

7 1/2 cups whole wheat flour

2–3 tablespoons cornmeal to sprinkle on pans

1. Generously grease (with butter or oil) two 9-x-5-inch bread pans, sprinkle generously with cornmeal, and set aside.

2. Place all of the ingredients in a large mixing bowl and beat well for 10 minutes with a wooden spoon, or use an electric mixer with a dough hook. (You are not going to knead this dough, so the beating and the rising are the only workouts it will get). Cover and set in a warm spot for 30 to 35 minutes, or until the dough almost doubles in bulk.

3. Poke the batter down with your fingers, cut it in half with a knife, and place in the prepared pans. Cover and set in a warm spot for about 40 to 45 minutes, or until the dough almost doubles in bulk (if using standard pans, it will not quite reach the tops).

4. Place the pans in a preheated 400°F oven and bake for about 50 minutes, or until the loaves are dark brown and hollow-sounding when rapped on the bottom with your knuckle. If the bread is even slightly soggy, put the loaves back into the oven directly on the oven rack and bake for another few minutes. Cool on a wire rack before serving.

FYI Batter breads rise very quickly and don't have to be kneaded, so they are great time savers. They can be made in about half the time it takes to make a kneaded bread.

TEN-GRAIN BREAD

If you love whole grain bread, this hearty loaf with its crunchy crust is sure to become one of your favorites. When preparing this recipe, it is easiest to use a ten-grain cereal, which you can find in most natural foods stores. I use Bob's Red Mill brand—it has wheat, corn, rye, triticale, oats and oat bran, soy, millet, barley, brown rice, and flaxseed. Of course, if you'd rather buy your own grains and grind them to a coarse, sand-like consistency, feel free.

1. Place the yeast, water, honey, salt, oil, cereal, and flaxseeds in a dishpan or large bowl and stir with a wooden spoon. Add the white flour, and beat with the spoon until well blended.

2. Add 3 cups of whole wheat flour, then squeeze the mixture with your hands until the flour disappears. If it is too wet to pick up, add more flour. As soon as you can handle the dough, sprinkle with a bit more flour and begin to knead directly in the bowl (or on a floured board), adding more flour as necessary. Knead for 10 minutes, or until the dough comes away from the sides of the bowl and your hands easily. (It will feel solid and somewhat less elastic than dough made from lighter bread mixtures.) Shape into a ball.

3. Spread a little oil on the bottom and sides of the bowl. Add the ball of dough, then turn it over, oiled side up. For this recipe, a slow rise is better than a quick one for good texture, so cover the bowl and set in a fairly cool spot for 40 to 60 minutes, or until the dough doubles in bulk. Lightly sprinkle a large baking sheet with cornmeal and set aside.

4. Punch down the risen dough, knead for 2 minutes, and form into a ball. Cut in half, then shape each half into a round loaf. Place the rounds on the prepared baking sheet, leaving enough space between them to allow for expansion. Let rise for 20 minutes.

5. Cut a $\frac{1}{2}$-inch-deep cross on the top of each risen loaf. Brush or spray the loaves with cold water, sprinkle the tops with flaxseeds, and place in a preheated 500°F oven. Spray the oven walls with cold water to create steam. Reduce the oven temperature to 400°F, and bake for 40 minutes, spraying the loaves and oven walls with cold water every 10 minutes. The loaves are ready when they are very dark brown and hollow-sounding when rapped on the bottom with your knuckle. Cool on a wire rack before serving.

**YIELD:
2 LARGE ROUNDS**

2 tablespoons (2 packets) active dry yeast

3 cups lukewarm water

2 tablespoons honey

1 tablespoon plus 2 teaspoons salt

4 tablespoons oil

1 $\frac{1}{2}$ cups uncooked 10-grain cereal

$\frac{1}{4}$ cup flaxseeds

1 cup unbleached white flour

5–6 cups whole wheat flour

1–2 tablespoons cornmeal for baking sheet

Flaxseeds to sprinkle on loaves

MULTIGRAIN BREAD

This hearty bread incorporates both ground and unground multigrain cereals, which are
readily available at natural food stores and most supermarkets. I use Country Choice
Multigrain Hot Cereal, which has whole flakes of unground barley, oats, and wheat, and
Bob's Red Mill 10-Grain Cereal, which contains ground wheat, corn, rye, triticale,
oats and oat bran, soy, millet, barley, brown rice, and flaxseed.

YIELD:
1 MEDIUM ROUND

1 tablespoon (1 packet)
  active dry yeast

1¼ cups lukewarm water

2 tablespoons oil

2 tablespoons honey

1 tablespoon salt

¾ cup uncooked *ground*
  multigrain cereal

2 cups unbleached white flour

1¼–1½ cups whole wheat flour

1 cup cooked *unground* cereal,
  cooled

Flakes of the *unground* cereal
  to sprinkle on loaf

1–2 tablespoons cornmeal
  for the baking sheet

1. Place the yeast, water, oil, honey, salt, and uncooked ground cereal in a dishpan or large bowl and stir with a wooden spoon. Add the white flour and 1 cup of whole wheat flour, and continue to stir with the spoon. Continue adding flour a bit at a time until you can't stir any more.

2. Add the cooled cooked cereal and begin to knead directly in the bowl (or on a floured board), adding more flour as necessary (the cereal will make the dough quite sticky). Knead for about 10 minutes, or until the dough is easy to handle and elastic. Shape into a ball.

3. Spread a little oil on the bottom and sides of the bowl. Add the ball of dough, then turn it over, oiled side up. Cover and set in a warm spot for about an hour, or until the dough doubles in size. Lightly sprinkle a large baking sheet with cornmeal and set aside.

4. Punch down the risen dough, knead for a minute, then let it rest for a few minutes. Shape into a round loaf and place on the prepared baking sheet. Cover and let rise about 30 minutes, or until doubled in bulk.

5. Brush or spray the loaf with cold water and sprinkle the top with *un*ground cereal flakes. Place in a preheated 400°F oven. Spray the oven walls with some cold water to create steam. Bake for 40 to 50 minutes, spraying the loaves and oven walls with cold water every 10 minutes. The bread is ready when it is browned and hollow-sounding when rapped on the bottom with your knuckle. Cool on a wire rack before serving.

OLIVE BREAD

Olive oil and Greek Calamata olives give this bread an
irresistibly piquant aroma and flavor.

1. Place the yeast and water in a dishpan or large bowl and stir with a wooden spoon. Add the white flour and 2 cups of whole wheat flour, and beat with the spoon until blended. Cover and let sit about 20 minutes, or until the top becomes bubbly. Stir in the salt, olive oil, olives, and more whole wheat flour, a little at a time, until you can't stir any more.

2. As soon as you can handle the dough, sprinkle with a bit more flour and begin to knead directly in the bowl (or on a floured board), adding more flour as necessary. Knead for about 10 minutes, or until the dough feels smooth and elastic. Shape into a ball.

3. Spread a little olive oil on the bottom and sides of the bowl. Add the ball of dough, then turn it over, oiled side up. Cover and set in a warm spot for about 50 minutes, or until the dough doubles in bulk. Punch down the risen dough and let rise a second time for about 30 minutes, or until doubled in bulk again. Lightly sprinkle a large baking sheet with cornmeal and set aside.

4. After the second rising, punch down the dough, knead for a minute, and form into a ball. Cut in half. Using both hands, pat each half into a torpedo-shaped loaf with a fat middle and gently tapered ends. Place the loaves on the prepared baking sheet, and let rest a couple minutes.

5. Cut a $\frac{1}{2}$-inch-deep slash lengthwise down the center of each loaf. Place in a preheated 400°F oven and bake for about 45 minutes, or until the bread is golden brown and hollow-sounding when rapped on the bottom with your knuckle. Cool on a wire rack before serving.

**YIELD:
2 MEDIUM LOAVES**

2 teaspoons active dry yeast

$2\frac{1}{2}$ cups lukewarm water

$1\frac{1}{2}$ cups unbleached
white flour

4–5 cups whole wheat flour

1 tablespoon salt

$\frac{1}{4}$ cup extra-virgin olive oil

1 cup pitted, very coarsely
chopped Calamata olives

1–2 tablespoons cornmeal
for the baking sheet

MULTI-SEED BREAD

*This great-looking bread, with a variety of seeds scattered over its crunchy top,
is a good choice for showcasing your skill as an artisan baker*

2 tablespoons (2 packets)
 active dry yeast

2½ cups lukewarm water

½ cup nonfat dry milk powder

2 tablespoons honey

2 tablespoons oil

1 tablespoon plus
 2 teaspoons salt

½ cup wheat germ

3 tablespoons sunflower seeds

3 tablespoons pumpkin seeds

3 tablespoons sesame seeds

2 tablespoons poppy seeds

2 cups unbleached white flour

4–6 cups whole wheat flour

1–2 tablespoons cornmeal
 for the baking sheet

Extra seeds to sprinkle
 on loaves

1. Place the yeast, water, milk powder, honey, oil, and salt in a dishpan or large bowl and stir with a wooden spoon. Add the wheat germ, sunflower seeds, pumpkin seeds, sesame seeds, poppy seeds, white flour, and 1 cup of whole wheat flour. Beat with the spoon until well blended.

2. Add 2 more cups of whole wheat flour, then squeeze the mixture with your hands until the flour disappears. If it is too wet to pick up, add a little more flour. As soon as you can handle the dough, sprinkle with a bit more flour and begin to knead directly in the bowl (or on a floured board), adding more flour as necessary. Knead for about 10 minutes, or until the dough leaves the sides of the bowl, is easy to handle, and elastic. Shape into a ball.

3. Spread a little oil on the bottom and sides of the bowl. Add the ball of dough, then turn it over, oiled side up. Cover and set in a warm spot for about an hour, or until the dough doubles in bulk. Lightly sprinkle a large baking sheet with cornmeal and set aside.

4. Punch down the risen dough, knead for a minute, and form into a ball. Cut in half, and shape each half into a round loaf. Place the loaves on the prepared baking sheet, leaving enough space between them to allow for expansion. Cut a ½-inch-deep cross on top of each loaf, spray or brush with cold water, and sprinkle with a mixture of seeds. Cover and let rise about 10 minutes.

5. Spray the loaves with cold water again. Place in a preheated 400°F oven, and set a pan of very hot water on the bottom rack (to create steam as the bread bakes). After 10 minutes, spray the loaves with cold water once again. Continue baking for another 30 minutes, or until the loaves are very brown and hollow-sounding when rapped on the bottom with your knuckle. Cool on a wire rack before serving.

WALNUT BREAD

Unlike many nut breads, this one is not sweet. It is, however, a wonderful all-purpose bread—great for sandwiches or for enjoying as is. It's also delicious toasted. Feel free to substitute other kinds of nuts for the walnuts. Try pecans, pistachios, or pine nuts.

1. Place the yeast and water in a dishpan or large bowl and stir with a wooden spoon until yeast is dissolved. Add the salt, white flour, and rye flour, and stir until well mixed. Cover and let sit at room temperature for about 20 minutes, or until the mixture begins to rise.

2. Add ½ cup of whole wheat flour, then squeeze the mixture with your hands until the flour disappears. If it is too wet to pick up, add a little more flour. As soon as you can handle the dough, sprinkle with a bit more flour and begin to knead directly in the bowl (or on a floured board), adding more flour as necessary. Knead for about 10 minutes, or until the dough is smooth and elastic. Flatten the dough, sprinkle with walnuts, and work them into the dough until well distributed. Shape the dough into a ball.

3. Spread a little oil on the bottom and sides of the bowl. Add the ball of dough, then turn it over, oiled side up. Cover and set in a warm spot for about an hour, or until the dough doubles in bulk. Thoroughly grease (with oil or butter) an 8-x-4-inch bread pan and set aside.

4. Punch down the risen dough, knead a minute, and form into a flattened rectangle that is a little longer than the pan. Starting at one of the long sides, tightly roll up the rectangle. Pinch the seam together, turn the loaf over, and tuck the ends under neatly. Place seam-side down in the prepared pan, cover, and let rise about 30 minutes, or until doubled in bulk.

5. Place the pan in a preheated 400°F oven and bake for about 50 minutes, or until the loaf is brown and hollow-sounding when rapped on the bottom with your knuckle. Cool on a wire rack before serving.

YIELD:
1 MEDIUM LOAF

- 1 tablespoon (1 packet) active dry yeast
- 1½ cups lukewarm water
- 1 tablespoon salt
- 1¾ cups unbleached white flour
- ½ cup rye flour
- ¾–1½ cups whole wheat flour
- 1 cup coarsely chopped walnuts

KAFFEE KLATCH BREAD

The small amounts of sugar and butter, while not enough to turn this bread into a pastry, are just enough to make it a particularly good snack to enjoy with a cup of coffee or tea.

YIELD:
1 MEDIUM LOAF

2 tablespoons sugar

1 teaspoon cinnamon

1 tablespoon (1 packet) active dry yeast

1½ cups lukewarm water

1 tablespoon salt

1¾ cups unbleached white flour

½ cup rye flour

¾–1½ cups whole wheat flour

1 cup coarsely chopped walnuts

2 tablespoons butter, at room temperature

1. Mix together the sugar and cinnamon in a small bowl and set aside.

2. Place the yeast and water in a dishpan or large bowl and stir with a wooden spoon. Add the salt, white flour, and rye flour, and stir until well mixed. Cover and let sit at room temperature for about 20 minutes, or until the mixture begins to rise.

3. Add ½ cup of whole wheat flour, then squeeze the mixture with your hands until the flour disappears. If it is too wet to pick up, add a little more flour. As soon as you can handle the dough, sprinkle with a bit more flour and begin to knead directly in the bowl (or on a floured board), adding more flour as necessary. Knead for about 10 minutes, or until the dough is smooth and elastic. Flatten the dough, sprinkle with walnuts and about three-fourths of the cinnamon-sugar mixture, and work into the dough until well distributed. Shape the dough into a ball.

4. Spread a little butter on the bottom and sides of the bowl. Add the ball of dough, then turn it over, buttered side up. Cover and set in a warm spot for about an hour, or until the dough doubles in bulk. Thoroughly butter an 8-x-4-inch bread pan and set aside.

5. Punch down the risen dough, knead for a minute, then form into a flattened rectangle that is a little longer than the pan. Starting at one of the long sides, tightly roll up the rectangle. Pinch the seam together, turn the loaf over, and tuck the ends under neatly. Place seam-side down in the prepared pan, cover, and let rise for 30 minutes, or until doubled in bulk.

6. Generously brush the top of the risen loaf with softened butter, and sprinkle with the remaining cinnamon-sugar. Place the pan in a preheated 400°F oven and bake for about 50 minutes, or until the loaf is brown and hollow-sounding when rapped on the bottom with your knuckle. Cool on a wire rack before serving.

5. Sourdough Breads

ourdough, the legendary bread of the Gold Rush days, still reigns supreme in San Francisco, as every tourist to that city knows. A bread like no other, it has a hearty rustic look, a thick crunchy crust, a chewy texture, and a distinctive and marvelous flavor.

Sourdough's special qualities are due to the fact that it is exactly what its name implies: sour dough. The dough goes through a fermentation process that results in a special tangy taste. The process begins with a starter: a mixture of flour and water that is exposed to the air until it captures some of the invisible wild yeast spores that abound in the atmosphere. There are hundreds of these strains floating in the air, and they impart their special flavors to the starter. Since there are so many variations, bakers love to argue over whose starter is the best. This chapter begins with instructions for making your own starter, but just in case you have no luck in catching some of that good wild yeast, a "foolproof" starter recipe is also provided.

Once you have created your starter, you can go on to the recipes for a classic sourdough bread and a sourdough rye. And, since these take longer to prepare than regular yeast breads, there is also a "cheater's" recipe for a quick sourdough version.

When preparing any sourdough bread, be aware that starters vary *very* widely in consistency, so you might need quite a bit more or less flour than the designated amount. Be extra careful when adding flour during kneading; start with about half the flour and then add more, a little at a time, as you work the dough. Stop adding flour as soon as it is no longer absorbed

Sourdough takes a lot of kneading (at least 10 minutes), but it is a very pleasant dough to work with. It quickly becomes smooth and tractable and it feels really good under your hands. To make the classic free-form loaves, you have to be sure the dough is stiff enough to hold its shape. To test the dough, put a blob on a greased pan or plate. If it flattens out, you need more flour.

Although big, round loaves of sourdough are the most familiar—and impressive—feel free to create any size or shape you fancy. You can make long thin baguettes, fat torpedo-shaped loaves, small or large rounds, whatever. Just place them on a baking sheet that has been sprinkled with cornmeal and bake.

Like most breads, sourdough freezes well. To restore the crisp crust during reheating, first let the bread thaw in its foil wrapper, then remove the foil and spray or sprinkle a little cold water on the top and sides. Pop the loaf into a preheated 400°F oven until it is warm and crisp.

No one can deny that making sourdough bread takes more time than any other bread. But once you bite into your first delectable slice, you'll be glad that you invested the extra minutes.

IT STARTS WITH A STARTER

Sourdough starter, like many other great developments, was the result of happenstance rather than scientific endeavor. When the first raised bread was made back in prehistoric times, it was probably because some distracted "baker" left the dough around too long and it began to ferment accidentally. In all likelihood, the baker was scared witless when the stuff began to rise, and he or she probably attributed the strange event to magic. We don't know how many times this "accidental" fermentation occurred before bakers connected it with deliciously flavored dough, nor do we know how long it took before someone figured out that it could be done on purpose. What we do know is that wild yeasts are always floating around in clean air, and that given the right medium and conditions, they will grow. It's easy enough to provide the medium and conditions; the tricky part is capturing the yeast.

During the days of the Gold Rush, prospectors who went West carried a bit of sourdough starter with them so they could bake bread over a campfire. The starter was a precious item, guarded like gold itself, for while every forty-niner knew how to make new starter (theoretically), it was always a chancy process and it also took more time than any hungry person wanted to wait. The formula for making the starter was simplicity itself—mix a cup of flour with a cup of water and wait for a wild airborne yeast to settle on the mixture. As soon as it began to bubble, the prospectors knew

they had captured the yeast. If they were remaining in one place, they used some of it to mix up a batch of dough and saved a cupful to start the next batch. But, if they were planning to move on, they waited for the dough to rise, and then removed a piece of the dough to use as starter for the next baking. Dough was certainly easier to transport than liquid and, given a little extra time, it worked just as well.

Nothing could be easier, right? Well, not exactly. You see, once in a while, the wild yeast just didn't come, or at least it didn't come quickly enough. Furthermore, there are a great number of undesirable molds that can also flourish in flour and water, spoiling the mixture and causing it to turn black, green, or some other unnerving color. When miners found that they were out of starter, they were known to walk any number of miles to a neighboring gulch to borrow some from fellow miners. A prudent prospector would make sure to keep his precious starter alive under all conditions—some went so far as to wear it in a little cloth bag under their shirts, hung from a string around their necks. It is said that some of San Francisco's famous sourdough breads are still made with starters that have been kept going since the Gold Rush days.

While you can certainly try making your own starter using the old prospectors' method, be aware that it is likely to work only in a location where the air is pure. In urban areas, there are apt to be more airborne pollutants than yeasts, but if you have patience (or you like to gamble), give it a try. You can also buy starter in most health food stores or from companies that sell it online or through mail order, but it's much more interesting to start your own.

Over the years, I have made a number of sourdough starters. The ones I have shared with you on the next page are the old prospectors' "Wild Yeast" method, and the less adventurous "Foolproof" method. But no matter which starter recipe or method you use, there are a few general guidelines that apply to all:

"Wild Yeast" Sourdough Starter

1. Place all of the ingredients in a glass or crockery container with a tightly fitting cover, and stir with a wooden spoon until well blended (don't bother making it smooth; the lumps will work themselves out). Cover the crock loosely with a paper towel and leave on the counter. Within a few hours, the mixture will begin to bubble.

2. Let the mixture sit for 3 to 5 days, or until it has a strong sour smell, a slight yellowish color, and the consistency of pancake batter.

3. Use the starter right away, or stir it (with a nonmetallic spoon), tightly close the container, and store in the refrigerator or freezer.

**YIELD:
ABOUT 3 CUPS**

2 cups lukewarm water

2 cups unbleached white flour

"Foolproof" Sourdough Starter

1. Follow the same directions as for the "Wild Yeast" Sourdough Starter (above). This one will be ready in about 3 days.

2. Use right away or store in the refrigerator or freezer.

**YIELD:
ABOUT 3 CUPS**

1 tablespoon (1 packet) active dry yeast

2 cups lukewarm water

2 cups unbleached white flour

❏ Starters can react to metal, so never use metal bowls or utensils during their preparation. Glass jars or mixing bowls and cramic crocks that can hold at least 1 quart and have tight-fitting covers are best, as are wooden or plastic spoons.

❏ Let the starter sit, loosely covered with a paper towel to keep out flies or other insects.

❏ It will begin to bubble in a few hours. Let it bubble away (ferment) for three to five days, until it has a strong sour smell. It is normal for a clear yellow liquid to form on top; just stir it back in once a day. If any other colors appear, the starter has attracted the wrong organisms. Throw it all away, scald the container, and start over.

❏ You will know the starter is ready by its good sour, yeasty smell, its slightly yellow color, and its pancake-batter consistency. It may also have grown in volume, which is why you started with a large container.

❏ Starter uses up its nutrients as it ferments, so you have to keep it alive by "feeding" it. Every time you use a cupful, add $\frac{1}{2}$ cup of fresh flour and $\frac{1}{2}$ cup of water (to equal the cup that was used) to the starter that's left in the container. Stir the mixture with a nonmetallic spoon, let it sit overnight at room temperature, then stir it again, cover tightly, and put it back in the fridge.

Starters improve with age, and once you have a really fine one going, it's a good idea to freeze some just in case the rest of the batch comes to grief. It can happen, because any active strain of yeast needs care and feeding. Even in the refrigerator, starter remains slightly active. Within a week or two it will use up all its nutrients and suffocate on the carbon dioxide gas it produces. You can prevent this tragedy with regular feeding. Here's how:

Whenever you don't use your starter for one week, stir it and pour out half (either give it or throw it away). Feed the remaining half by adding a half cup each of flour and water. Stir with a nonmetallic spoon and leave it out overnight before refrigerating.

Each of the bread recipes in this chapter requires one cup of starter. As the following starter recipes yield three or more cups, you can use one cup for the recipe and save the rest for later use. After you have fed and stored your starter, *you will have to remember to feed it weekly!*

QUICK SOURDOUGH BREAD

If you have some starter in your refrigerator or freezer, you might consider making this quick sourdough bread. It is a compromise, containing starter for flavor and dry yeast for speed. Although it is not quite as extraordinary as the real thing, you can make it in a few hours—and with that advantage, you may well prefer it. For added nutrition, you can substitute some whole wheat flour for the white.

1. Place the yeast, water, starter, sugar, and salt in a dishpan or large bowl and stir with a wooden spoon. Add 4 cups of flour and beat with the spoon for a minute until well blended. Cover and let sit in a warm spot for about an hour, or until doubled in bulk. Sprinkle a large baking sheet with cornmeal and set aside.

2. Add 2 more cups of flour and begin to knead directly in the bowl (or on a floured board), adding more flour as necessary. Knead for 8 to 10 minutes, or until the dough is smooth and elastic. Shape into a ball.

3. Cut the dough in half, then shape each half into a round loaf. Place the loaves on the prepared baking sheet, leaving enough space between them to allow for expansion. Cover and let rise about 40 minutes, or until doubled in bulk.

4. Cut a $\frac{1}{2}$-inch-deep cross on top of each risen loaf. Spray or brush the tops with cold water and place in a cold oven. Turn on the oven to 400°F, and set a pan of very hot water on the bottom rack (to create steam as the bread bakes).

5. Spraying often with cold water, bake the loaves for 45 minutes, or until golden brown and hollow-sounding when rapped on the bottom with your knuckle. Cool on a wire rack before serving.

YIELD:
2 LARGE ROUNDS

1 tablespoon (1 packet) active dry yeast

$1\frac{1}{2}$ cups lukewarm water

1 cup premade sourdough starter, at room temperature (recipe on page 75)

1 tablespoon sugar

1 tablespoon salt

6–7 cups unbleached white flour

CLASSIC SOURDOUGH BREAD

Sourdough is not a spur-of-the-moment bread. It's best to allow yourself a full twenty-four hours,
although it may not take that long. I always find mid-afternoon a convenient time to begin a
sourdough batch; you will have bread in time for dinner the next night. Begin the procedure by
"setting the sponge," a fancy term that means giving your starter a good feeding and letting
it grow. The longer the sponge sits around, the more sour and tasty your bread will be.

YIELD: 2 LARGE ROUNDS

THE SPONGE

1 cup sourdough starter*
(see page 75)

2 cups lukewarm water

3 cups unbleached
white flour

THE BREAD

1 tablespoon sugar

2 tablespoons oil

1 tablespoon salt

4–5 cups unbleached
white flour

*When you take out your cupful of starter, remember to feed the remaining batch by stirring in ½ cup water and ½ cup flour. Leave out overnight before refrigerating again.

1. Mix all of the sponge ingredients in a medium-size bowl and cover with plastic wrap or a clean dishtowel. Let sit at room temperature for at least 12 hours, or until the sponge doubles in bulk and has a bubbly top.

2. Stir the sponge and transfer it to a dishpan or large bowl. Add the sugar, oil, salt, and 2 cups of flour, and stir with a wooden spoon for a minute until well blended. Keep sprinkling in flour and, when you can't stir anymore, start to mix with your hands. Continue to add flour as necessary, a bit at a time.

3. As soon as you can handle the dough, begin to knead directly in the bowl (or on a floured board), adding sprinkles of flour until the dough doesn't absorb any more. Knead for at least 10 minutes, or until the dough is smooth and elastic. Shape into a ball.

4. Spread a little oil on the bottom and sides of the bowl. Add the ball of dough, and then turn it over, oiled side up. Cover and set in a warm spot for about an hour, or until the dough doubles in bulk. Lightly sprinkle a large baking sheet with cornmeal and set aside.

5. Punch down the risen dough, knead for a minute, and form into a ball. Cut in half, then shape each half into a round loaf. Place the loaves on the prepared baking sheet, leaving enough space between them to allow for expansion. Cover and let rise about 45 minutes, or until doubled in bulk. (This may take more or less time, depending on how active the starter is.)

6. Cut a $\frac{1}{2}$-inch-deep cross on top of each risen loaf. Mix a half-cup of cold water with a pinch of salt, and spray or brush some on each. Place in a pre-heated 400°F oven, and set a pan of very hot water on the bottom rack (to create steam as the bread bakes).

7. Spraying often with cold water, bake the loaves for 50 minutes, or until golden brown and hollow-sounding when rapped on the bottom with your knuckle. Cool on a wire rack before serving.

VARIATION

Sourdough Whole Wheat Bread Make the sponge as instructed, but use all or part whole wheat flour for the bread instead of unbleached white.

TIP If, by mistake, you have used up all your starter, use a little of the sponge to start a new batch. Place a cup of the sponge in a crock or glass jar, and stir in enough flour and water in approximately equal parts to total 2 cups. Cover the mixture loosely and let it sit at room temperature for 12 hours. Cover and refrigerate or freeze.

SOURDOUGH RYE BREAD

This is it—the real thing. Jewish Rye, Deli Rye, New York Rye; whatever you call it,
this is the incomparable caraway-flecked loaf with the crisp crust and soft interior.
The only kind of bread in the world that's right with pastrami and a pickle.

YIELD:
2 LARGE OVAL LOAVES

THE SPONGE

1 cup sourdough starter*
   (see page 75)

2 cups lukewarm water

4 tablespoons oil

2 tablespoons molasses

2 cups rye flour

2 cups unbleached white flour

THE BREAD

1 tablespoon salt

$\frac{1}{2}$ teaspoon baking soda

1 tablespoon caraway seeds

1 cup rye flour

2–3 cups unbleached white flour

1 egg white plus
   1 tablespoon cold water

FYI Be aware that the dough for this recipe is not easy to knead. Rye flour is deficient in gluten and very sticky, so you will have to work the white flour extra hard to make its gluten strong enough to "carry along" the rye flour.

1. Mix all of the sponge ingredients in a large bowl and cover with plastic wrap or a clean dishtowel. Let sit at room temperature for at least 12 hours, or until the sponge doubles in bulk and has a bubbly top.

2. Stir the sponge and transfer it to a dishpan or large bowl. Add the salt, baking soda, caraway seeds, rye flour, and 2 cups of white flour. Beat with a wooden spoon until well blended. Continue to sprinkle more flour on the doughy batter until you can't stir anymore, then start to mix with your hands. Add more flour a bit at a time, as necessary.

3. As soon as you can handle the dough, sprinkle lightly with more white flour and begin to knead directly in the bowl (or on a floured board), adding more flour a little at a time until the dough doesn't absorb any more. Knead for a full 10 minutes (and don't cheat), or until the dough is smooth and elastic. Shape into a ball. Lightly sprinkle a large baking sheet with cornmeal and set aside.

4. Cut the ball of dough in half, then shape each half into an oval loaf. Place the loaves on the prepared baking sheet, leaving enough space between them to allow for expansion. Cover and set in a warm spot for about 2 hours, or until the loaves have doubled in bulk.

5. Cut three $\frac{1}{2}$-inch-deep slashes diagonally across the top of each risen loaf. In a small bowl, beat together the egg white and cold water, then brush some on each loaf. Sprinkle with caraway seeds, and place in a preheated 375°F oven. After 30 minutes, brush the loaves with more egg white mixture, and continue to bake another 20 minutes, or until the loaves are browned and hollow-sounding when rapped on the bottom with your knuckle. Cool on a wire rack before serving.

*When you take out your cupful of starter, remember to feed the remaining batch by stirring in $\frac{1}{2}$ cup water and $\frac{1}{2}$ cup flour. Leave out overnight before refrigerating again.

6. Sweet Yeast Breads

Sweet yeast breads, as their name implies, are not dinner or sandwich breads. They are actually very light pastries and are appropriate for dessert, teatime, breakfast treats, and snacks. They include such favorites as Crumb Cake, Caramel Rolls (*Schnecken*), Turnovers (with various mouth-watering fillings), Swedish Tea Ring, and Hot Cross Buns.

All of these breads are made with one basic and very versatile sweet-dough recipe that lends itself to a variety of shapes and sizes. It readily accepts such enhancements as spices, jam, nuts, fruits, and icing to produce a great assortment of luscious pastries.

And, as an added bonus, you will find this dough extremely easy to work with right from the start. Unlike some of the heavier bread doughs, it doesn't take much kneading before it is smooth, bouncy, and ready to go. The baking time is fairly short, too, often only twenty minutes.

Among the other indulgences included in this chapter is a trio of festive sweet yeast breads—breads traditionally made by people in different parts of the world to celebrate special holidays. For Christmas there is rich, fruity Panettone from Italy and Stollen from Germany; for Easter, Russian Kulich. These breads are not made with the basic Sweet Yeast Dough recipe and they are a little more complex than the everyday sweet breads. Although they are very special breads for very special occasions, they are still fairly easy to make—and, if they take just a little more time and trouble, they are definitely well worth it.

BASIC SWEET YEAST DOUGH

This sweet yeast dough is basic in the same sense that the dough for Basic White Bread (page 32) is basic—it serves as the basis for a great variety of buns and coffee cakes, including a number of recipes found in this chapter. If you like, you can easily double (or even triple) this recipe, use a portion, and refrigerate the rest.

YIELD: See individual recipes (Pages 83–91)

1 tablespoon (1 packet) active dry yeast

½ cup lukewarm water

⅓ cup nonfat dry milk powder

4 tablespoons sugar

½ teaspoon salt

4 tablespoons very soft butter

2 eggs

2–2½ cups unbleached white flour

1. Place all of the ingredients except the flour in a large mixing bowl* and stir with a wooden spoon. Add 2 cups of the flour and continue to stir, adding more flour a little at a time, until you can handle the dough.

2. Sprinkle the dough with flour and begin to knead directly in the bowl (or on a floured board), adding more flour as necessary. Knead for about 5 minutes, or until the dough is smooth and elastic. Shape into a ball.

3. Wash the bowl and butter its bottom and sides generously. Add the ball of dough, then turn it over, buttered side up. Cover and set in a warm spot for about an hour, or until the dough doubles in bulk.

4. Punch down the risen dough. It is now ready to use (see recipes on pages 83 through 91) or store for later use. To store, simply form the dough into a ball, butter the outside, and place in a plastic bag (the butter will keep the dough from sticking to the bag). Store in the refrigerator, where it will keep for three or four days. Be aware that it will probably rise a little, so be sure to punch it down before using.

* If you are making a single recipe, you can use an ordinary large mixing bowl; if you are going to double or triple the recipe, consider the dishpan method (page 17) for mixing the ingredients and kneading the dough.

JAM BUNS

Not too fancy, not too sweet. Embellished only with a spoonful of jam and a sprinkle of sugar, these buns are especially nice for breakfast or a coffee break.

1. Place the dough on a lightly floured board and roll into a ½-inch thick rectangle or square. Using a floured 3-inch biscuit cutter or rim of a glass, cut circles from the dough and place on a well-greased baking sheet, leaving enough room between them to allow for expansion.

2. Using your thumb, make a deep well in the center of each circle of dough. Fill the well with a heaping teaspoon of jam. Let rise until the buns have more than doubled in size.

3. Beat the egg white with a small whisk or fork until it forms soft peaks, then brush some on top of each risen bun. Sprinkle with confectioner's sugar (you can shake it through a small sieve).

4. Place the buns in a preheated 375°F oven and bake for 20 minutes, or until browned. Cool on a wire rack.

> **YIELD: ABOUT 12 BUNS**
>
> Basic Sweet Yeast Dough (page 82)
>
> ¼–½ cup fruit jam
>
> 1 egg white
>
> Confectioner's sugar to sprinkle on top

Cut 3-inch circles from the dough.

Place a teaspoon of jam on each circle.

Brush with beaten egg white and sprinkle with confectioner's sugar.

SWEDISH TEA RING

*A few slashes with your scissors and a flip of your wrist turn this easy-to-make ring
into an impressive professional-looking creation.*

**YIELD:
10 SERVINGS**

Basic Sweet Yeast Dough
(page 82)

2 tablespoons softened butter

$\frac{1}{2}$ cup brown sugar

2 teaspoons cinnamon

$\frac{1}{2}$ cup raisins, currants, or
mixture of both

ICING

1 cup confectioner's sugar

About 1 tablespoon milk

Few drops vanilla extract or
other flavor, such as almond,
lemon, or orange

1. Place the dough on a lightly floured board and roll into a rectangle
about 8-x-16 inches. Spread the dough with softened butter, then sprinkle
the brown sugar, cinnamon, and fruit evenly on top.

2. Starting at one of the long sides, carefully roll up the dough like a
jellyroll, keeping it as even as possible. Pinch the seam together tightly.
(If necessary, carefully shape and pull the roll until it is fairly even in
diameter.)

3. Carefully lift the roll onto a greased baking sheet, seam-side down.
Join the ends to form a ring and pinch closed. With kitchen shears (or any
large clean scissors), make cuts along the outer edge of the ring. The cuts
should be about 1 inch apart and a little deeper than halfway into the roll.

4. After making the cuts, gently lift each "petal" (without ripping it
from the ring) and turn on its side. Cover and set in a warm spot for about
45 minutes, or until doubled in size.

5. Place in a preheated 375°F oven and bake for 20 to 25 minutes, or
until well browned. Set the baking sheet on a wire rack and let the ring cool.

6. To prepare the icing, stir together the confectioner's sugar, milk, and
vanilla in a small bowl until very smooth. If it is too thick, add more milk,
one drop at a time, until the desired consistency is reached. If too thin, add
more confectioner's sugar, 1 tablespoon at a time. Spread or drizzle the icing
over the cooled ring. Allow the icing to set about 20 minutes before serving.

TIP After icing the ring (and while the icing is still soft), you can
further decorate your already beautiful Swedish Tea Ring
with a sprinkling of chopped nuts or candied fruit.

Spread the filling over the dough.

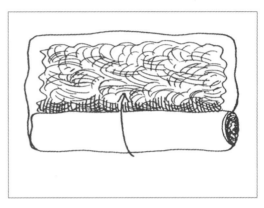

Roll up the dough from one of the long sides.

Join the ends of the roll to form a ring.

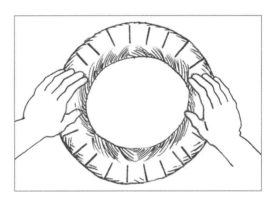

Make cuts about an inch apart and a little deeper than halfway into the roll.

Gently lift each "petal" and turn on its side.

CARAMEL ROLLS (SCHNECKEN)

"Schnecken" is the German word for snails, but these "snails" are luscious sticky buns.

Basic Sweet Yeast Dough
(page 82)

TOPPING

8 tablespoons (1 stick) butter

½ cup brown sugar

½ cup broken pecans or
sliced almonds

FILLING

2 tablespoons softened butter

1–2 teaspoons cinnamon

½ cup raisins (optional)

1. For the topping, melt the butter in a 10-inch-round cake pan (or skillet with a heatproof handle). Add the brown sugar, stir well, and spread the mixture in an even layer on the bottom of the pan. Sprinkle the nuts on top. Set aside.

Spread the filling over the dough.

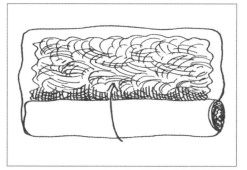

Roll up the dough from one of the long sides.

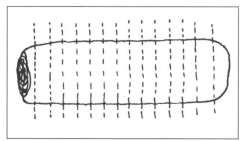

Cut the roll into 1-inch slices.

2. Place the dough on a lightly floured board and roll into a rectangle about 8-x-16 inches. For the filling, spread the dough with softened butter and sprinkle with cinnamon and raisins (if using) evenly on top.

3. Starting at one of the long sides, carefully roll up the dough like a jellyroll, keeping it as even as possible. Pinch the seam together tightly, and set the roll seam-side down on the board.

4. Cut the roll into roughly 1-inch slices (if the ends of the rolls are scraggly, cut them off and discard before you begin slicing). Place the slices cut side down in the cake pan on top of the brown sugar-butter mixture. Cover and let rise about 45 minutes or more, until doubled in size. The rolls will all be touching each other.

5. Place in a preheated 350°F oven and bake for about 40 minutes, or until the rolls are well browned. Remove the pan from the oven, place a large plate on top, and invert to turn out the rolls. Let cool before serving.

Place the slices cut side down in the pan.

CRUMB CAKE

The butter and sugar in the topping combine to give this simple cake a rich, sweet, crumbly crust.

1. Press the dough into a buttered 8-x-8-inch pan.

2. Mix all of the topping ingredients together with your fingertips until well blended and crumbly. Sprinkle the mixture evenly over the top of the dough. Cover and set in a warm spot for about 45 minutes, or until the dough doubles in bulk.

3. Place in a preheated 375°F oven for about 20 minutes, or until well browned. Let cool in the pan on a wire rack before serving.

**YIELD:
8-INCH SQUARE CAKE**

Basic Sweet Yeast Dough (page 32)

TOPPING

½ cup white flour

⅓ cup sugar

1 teaspoon cinnamon

4 tablespoons (½ stick) soft butter

HOT CROSS BUNS

Traditional during the Lenten season, these plain buns are good any time.
When you're not in the mood for "plain," try them with butter, cream cheese, or jam.

Basic Sweet Yeast Dough (page 82),
   prepared through Step 1

½ cup currants

1–2 tablespoons melted butter

½ cup milk

1 tablespoon sugar

ICING

1 cup confectioner's sugar

About 1 tablespoon milk

Few drops vanilla extract or other flavor,
   such as almond, lemon, or orange

1. Before kneading the Basic Sweet Yeast Dough, add the currants. Knead for 5 minutes, or until the dough is elastic, then shape into a ball. Butter the bottom and sides of the mixing bowl, add the ball of dough, then turn it over, buttered side up. Cover and set in a warm spot for about an hour, or until the dough doubles in bulk. Butter a 10-inch round cake pan and set aside.

2. Punch down the risen dough. Pull off pieces and shape into small rounds the size of Ping-Pong balls (there will be about 12 to15). Place them fairly close together (but not touching) in the prepared cake pan. Brush the tops with melted butter, and let sit 30 minutes or more, or until they just begin to rise.

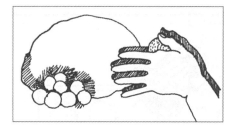

Pull off pieces of dough and form into
rounds the size of Ping-Pong balls.

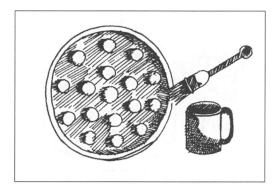

Place the balls close together in the pan,
but not touching.

3. Cut a ½-inch deep cross into the top of each partially risen ball, cover, and let continue to rise until they have more than doubled their original size. Place in a preheated 375°F oven and bake for about 20 minutes, or until the balls have browned. Remove the pan from the oven and set aside.

4. In a small bowl, mix together the milk and sugar, then brush some on top of the hot buns. Return them to the oven for another 2 minutes. Remove the buns and place on a wire rack to cool completely.

5. To prepare the icing, stir together the confectioner's sugar, milk, and vanilla in a small bowl until very smooth. If too thick, add more milk, one drop at a time, until the desired consistency is reached. If too thin, add more confectioner's sugar, 1 tablespoon at a time. Spoon the icing into the cross on top of each bun. Allow the icing to set for 20 minutes before serving.

Cut crosses into each partially risen ball.

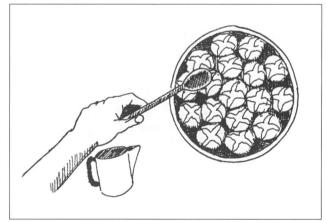

Spoon icing into the crosses on top of the cooled buns.

TURNOVERS

Turnovers are like miniature pies with luscious hidden fillings. In addition to the filling variations provided here, you can use any fruit pie filling or even applesauce.

**YIELD:
12 TURNOVERS**

Basic Sweet Dough
(page 82)

Filling of choice
(see recipes on next page)

1. Prepare one of the turnover fillings and set aside.

2. Place the dough on a lightly floured board and roll into a $\frac{1}{2}$-inch thick rectangle or square. Cut the dough into 12 squares (about 3-inches). Place 1 tablespoon of filling in the center of each square. Lift one corner and fold it over the filling to meet the opposite corner and form a triangle. Dab a little cold water on the inside edges of the dough (to make sure the sides stick), then pinch the sides together securely. (Alternatively, you can raise all four corners and pinch them together in the center, above the filling.)

3. Transfer the turnovers to a greased baking sheet, leaving enough room between them to allow for expansion. Cover and let rise for 45 minutes, or until doubled in bulk.

4. Place in a preheated 400°F oven and bake for 20 to 30 minutes, or until the turnovers are well browned. (Baking time will vary depending on the filling.) Cool on a wire rack before serving.

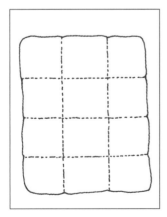

Cut the dough into
12 squares.

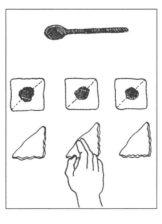

Spoon filling in the center
of each square.

Transfer the triangles
to a baking sheet.

FILLING CHOICES

WALNUT FILLING

2 cups ground or chopped walnuts

$1/4$ cup sugar

$1/4$ cup honey

Mix all the ingredients together to form a nutty paste.

PRUNE FILLING

1 pound prunes

1/2 cup sugar

1 tablespoon lemon juice

Boil the prunes in a little water until very soft. Remove the pits (if any), then rub the prunes through a colander or purée them in a food processor. Mix the purée with the sugar and lemon juice.

APRICOT FILLING

1 pound dried apricots

$1/2$ cup sugar

1 tablespoon lemon juice

Boil the apricots in a little water until very soft. Remove the pits (if any), then rub the apricots through a colander or purée them in a food processor. Mix the purée with the sugar and lemon juice.

ALMOND FILLING

$1/2$ cup ground or finely chopped almonds

3 tablespoons butter, at room temperature

1 teaspoon grated lemon rind

1 egg, beaten

Mix the almonds, butter, and lemon rind together. Add enough of the egg to form a stiff paste.

STOLLEN

This version of the traditional German Christmas bread is particularly rich and fruity.

**YIELD:
1 LARGE LOAF**

$3/4$ cup sugar

1 stick ($1/2$ cup) soft butter, divided

2 eggs

2 tablespoons (2 packets)
    active dry yeast

$1/3$ cup nonfat dry milk powder

$1/2$ teaspoon salt

1 cup lukewarm water

1 teaspoon almond extract

2 cups whole wheat flour

3–4 cups unbleached white flour

$1/2$ cup sliced or chopped almonds

1 tablespoon grated orange peel

1 tablespoon grated lemon peel

2 tablespoons melted butter

Confectioner's sugar to sprinkle
    on top

FRUIT MIXTURE

$1/2$ cup raisins

$1/2$ cup currants

2 cups diced candied fruits

$1/2$ cup rum or brandy

1. Place all the fruit mixture ingredients in a small bowl and let stand for 30 minutes.

2. Place the sugar and $3/4$ stick (6 tablespoons) of the butter in a large bowl and blend with a wooden spoon. Add the eggs, yeast, milk powder, salt, lukewarm water, and almond extract, and beat until well blended. Add the whole wheat flour and $2^1/2$ cups white flour. Beat with the spoon, adding more flour a little at a time until you can handle the dough.

3. Sprinkle the dough with a little flour and begin to knead directly in the bowl (or on a floured board), adding more flour as necessary. Knead for about 5 minutes, or until the dough is smooth and elastic. Shape into a ball.

4. Wash and dry the bowl, butter it, and add the dough ball. Turn it over, cover, and set in a warm place for about an hour, or until doubled in bulk. Thoroughly butter a baking sheet and set aside.

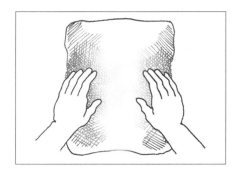

Pat the dough into a rectangle.

5. Punch down the risen dough and flatten it out with your fingers. Top with the fruit mixture (and its liquid), the almonds, and the grated orange and lemon peel, and work them into the dough until well distributed. Pat the dough into a rectangle about 8-x-16 inches and spread the remaining butter on top. Fold one of the long sides to the center, then fold the other side to the center so that it overlaps just a bit. Pinch the seam together and taper the ends neatly. If some of the fruit falls out, just stick it on top.

6. Using two wide spatulas, carefully transfer the stollen to the prepared baking sheet. Cover and let rise for about an hour, or until doubled in bulk.

7. Brush the top with melted butter. Place in a preheated 375°F oven and bake for 40 minutes, or until well browned. Remove from the oven and let cool on the baking sheet. While the stollen is still warm, dust with confectioner's sugar. When it has cooled completely, dust again (once or twice) with confectioner's sugar.

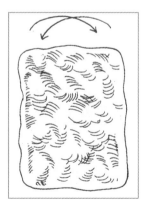

Fold both long sides
to the center.

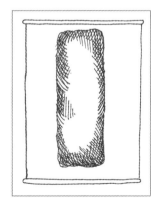

Transfer the prepared
dough to a baking sheet.

KULICH

This tall Russian Orthodox Easter bread is covered with white icing, making it look like a snow-covered mountain. When the bread (which is really more like a cake) is served, the top is cut off in a single slice and then replaced, so that even as the loaf grows shorter, it always looks complete. Truly traditional kulich has the initials XV (for "Christ is Risen") on top. To do this, save a little dough, roll it into a thin rope, and form the letters.

YIELD:
1 LARGE LOAF

¼ cup golden raisins

¼ cup dark raisins

2 tablespoons sherry

6 tablespoons soft butter

½ cup lukewarm water

¼ cup sugar

1 teaspoon salt

1 egg

1 tablespoon (1 packet) active dry yeast

1 teaspoon grated lemon peel

2–3 cups unbleached white flour

¼ cup sliced or chopped almonds

ICING

½ cup confectioner's sugar

1½ teaspoon milk or cream

1. Place the raisins and sherry in a small bowl and set aside.

2. Put the butter into a large mixing bowl, add the lukewarm water, sugar, salt, egg, yeast, lemon peel, and about 1½ cups flour. Beat with the spoon until well blended. Add the soaked raisins (and their liquid), almonds, and more flour a little at a time, until you can handle the dough.

3. Sprinkle the dough with a little flour and begin to knead directly in the bowl (or on a floured board), adding more flour as necessary. Knead for about 5 minutes, or until the dough is smooth and elastic. Shape into a ball, cover, and set in a warm place for at least an hour, or until doubled in bulk. Thoroughly butter a 2-pound metal coffee can, and sprinkle the bottom and sides well with cornmeal.

Cut off a small piece of dough.

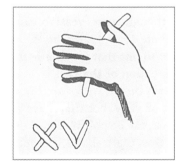

Roll the small piece of dough into slender ropes to form the initials "XV."

4. Punch down the risen dough and knead for a minute or so. If putting the initials "XV" on top of the bread, take a little dough and form the letters. Shape the remaining dough into a ball and drop it into the prepared coffee can. Cover and let rise for at least an hour, or until the dough rises to reach the top of the can. If adding the initials, place them on top.

5. Place the can in a preheated 350°F oven and bake for 45 to 50 minutes, or until a skewer (a toothpick will be too short) inserted into the center of the bread comes out clean. Turn the bread out of the can and place on a wire rack to cool.

6. To prepare the icing, stir together the confectioner's sugar and milk in a small bowl until very smooth and just thin enough to spread on top of the kulich and let drip down the sides. If too thick, add more milk, one drop at a time, to reach the desired consistency. If too thin, add more confectioner's sugar, 1 tablespoon at a time. After frosting the kulich, allow the icing to set for 20 minutes before serving.

Drop the remaining dough into the prepared coffee can, cover, and let rise.

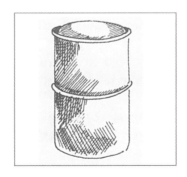

Let the dough rise until it reaches the top of the can.

Spoon the icing on top of the cooled cake, letting it drip down the sides.

PANETTONE

Panettone, or fruit bread, is a traditional Christmas treat in Italy, but this version is somewhat untraditional—it's a batter bread that requires no kneading. Rich, sweet, and equally good whether made with white or whole wheat flour, panettone is more of a pastry than a bread. You can leave the loaf plain or spread a little honey on top and sprinkle with blanched, sliced almonds.

**YIELD:
1 LARGE LOAF**

½ cup (1 stick) soft butter

¾ cup brown sugar

3 eggs

2 tablespoons (2 packets) active dry yeast

⅓ cup nonfat dry milk powder

1½ cups lukewarm water

1 teaspoon salt

3½ cups whole wheat or white unbleached flour

2 teaspoons anise powder*

¼ cup brandy, rum, or Marsala wine

1 cup diced, mixed candied fruit

¼ cup currants

* Also sold as star anise powder.

1. Cream together the butter and sugar in a large mixing bowl with a wooden spoon or in an electric mixer. Separate the eggs and add the yolks to the bowl along with all the remaining ingredients except the candied fruit and currants. Beat well for 2 minutes, then stir in the candied fruit and currants.

2. Beat the egg whites until they form stiff peaks, then fold into the batter. Cover the bowl and set in a warm spot for about an hour or more, or until the batter is light and frothy, and almost doubled in bulk. Stir down the batter and pour it into a well-buttered 9-inch tube or springform pan. Cover and let rise for about an hour, or until the batter reaches the top of the pan.

3. Place the pan in a preheated 375°F oven. Bake for 30 minutes, then lower the heat to 325°F. Bake for another 20 minutes, or until a toothpick inserted into the center of the bread comes out clean.

4. Remove the pan from the oven and let sit 5 minutes before removing the bread. Cool the bread on a wire rack before serving.

7. Quick Breads, Biscuits, and Muffins

Although some yeast breads can be made in relatively little time, the term "quick bread" never refers to yeast bread, but rather to one that is leavened with baking powder, baking soda, or a combination of the two. Quick breads are less exciting than yeast breads from the baker's point of view, but they have some very definite advantages. All can be prepared in about one hour (some in much less time). They are all easy to make and offer tremendous variety.

In this chapter, you will find quick breads that go along with meals, such as melt-in-your mouth Down-Home Biscuits—as good as any you've ever tasted; an authentic Irish Soda Bread that is studded with currants; and moist and crumbly Yellow Corn Bread with just a hint of sweetness. There are also muffins of every persuasion—including Bran, Blueberry, Whole Wheat, and Chocolate Chocolate Chip. Also included are quick breads that make fine desserts, such as the sweet and spicy Carrot Bread and the rich Cranberry Nut Bread. And can you think of anything more traditional (and pleasing) with tea than a hot buttered scone? Some of the following recipes have seasonal significance, too. Pumpkin Bread is especially appropriate to serve during the harvest season, and Zucchini Bread is a summertime blessing for all whose gardens are overflowing with more of this vegetable than they can ever hope to eat.

Be aware that because quick breads tend to be crumbly, they do not lend themselves well to sandwiches, but most make excellent toast. And since they do not require kneading, you won't need your dishpan during their preparation—just use an ordinary mixing bowl.

YELLOW CORN BREAD

Yellow corn bread is the Northern or Yankee variety—thick, moist, and slightly sweet.
It is best baked to order and served steaming hot.

**YIELD:
9 SERVINGS**

1 cup unbleached white flour

¼ cup sugar

4 teaspoons baking powder

¾ teaspoon salt

1 cup yellow cornmeal

1 cup milk

2 eggs

4 tablespoons (½ stick)
   soft butter

1. Preheat the oven to 425°F. Generously butter a 9-inch square cake pan and set aside.

2. Place the flour, sugar, baking powder, salt, and cornmeal in a large mixing bowl and stir with a wooden spoon until blended. Add the milk, eggs, and butter, and stir just long enough to moisten the dry ingredients—do not overstir. The batter will remain somewhat lumpy.

3. Pour the batter into the prepared pan and bake for 20 to 25 minutes, or until a toothpick inserted in the center comes out clean. Be careful not to overbake since corn bread has a tendency to become dry.

4. Cut into 3-inch squares and serve steaming hot right from the pan.

FYI Unlike yeast dough, baking powder batter should be handled as little as possible. This means don't overstir the batter—mix just until the flour disappears (there will be small lumps in the batter, but don't try to get rid of them). Get the filled pan into the oven as quickly as possible.

SCOTTISH SODA BREAD

A tender, crumbly, biscuit-like bread that can be started an hour before mealtime.
To serve, break off chunks from the loaf, but if there is any left over, slice it for breakfast toast.

1. Preheat the oven to 375°F. Sprinkle flour on any round or square cake pan or pie plate and set aside.

2. Place the flour, sugar, baking powder, baking soda, salt, and caraway seeds (if using) in a large mixing bowl. Add the butter and work it in with your fingertips until the mixture is crumbly and even in texture. Add the buttermilk and stir with a wooden spoon just long enough to moisten the dry ingredients.

3. Knead the mixture in the bowl for a minute. (The purpose of the kneading is not to develop gluten, as with yeast dough, but simply to mix the dough thoroughly — so don't overdo it.) If the dough is too sticky to handle, add a little more flour.

4. Shape the dough into a ball about 8 inches in diameter and place on the prepared pan. Dip a sharp knife in flour and use it to make two deep cuts into the loaf (almost — but not quite — to the bottom) in the shape of a plus sign. As the bread bakes, the cuts will spread apart.

5. Bake for about 30 to 40 minutes, or until the bread is golden brown and spread out like an open flower. Cool on a wire rack. To serve, pull the bread apart at the cut lines and tear off pieces.

**YIELD:
1 MEDIUM ROUND**

$2\frac{1}{2}$ cups unbleached white flour

2 teaspoons sugar

2 teaspoons baking powder

1 teaspoon baking soda

$\frac{1}{2}$ teaspoon salt

1 tablespoon caraway seeds (optional)

3 tablespoons soft butter

1 cup buttermilk*

* As a substitute, you can use plain yogurt.

IRISH SODA BREAD

Similar to the Scottish version in form, Irish soda bread is richer and sweeter, making it better suited to enjoy at breakfast or teatime. Some experts claim that the Irish country folk always make this bread with whole wheat flour. Not surprisingly, it makes a coarser, heavier product, but you might try it and see which version you prefer. I like it best with half white, half whole wheat rather than all of one or the other.

YIELD:
2 MEDIUM LOAVES

5 cups unbleached white flour

4 tablespoons sugar

1 teaspoon salt

1 teaspoon baking powder

1 teaspoon baking soda

4 tablespoons (½ stick)
   soft butter

1¾ cups buttermilk*

1 egg, beaten

1 cup currants

* As a substitute, you can use plain yogurt.

1. Preheat the oven to 375°F. Sprinkle some flour on a large baking sheet and set aside.

2. Place the flour, sugar, salt, baking powder, and baking soda in a large mixing bowl. Add the butter and work it in with your fingertips until the mixture is crumbly and even in texture. Make a well in the center, pour in the buttermilk, and add the egg. Beat the egg into the buttermilk until it is well blended, then continue to stir with a wooden spoon just long enough to moisten the dry ingredients.

3. Add the currants, then knead the mixture to distribute them evenly. (The purpose of the kneading is not to develop gluten, as with yeast dough, so don't overdo it.) If the dough is too sticky to handle, add a little more flour.

4. Cut the dough in half and shape each half into a ball. Place the balls on the prepared baking sheet, leaving enough space between them to allow for expansion. Dip a sharp knife in flour and use it to make two deep cuts into each loaf (almost—but not quite—to the bottom) in the shape of a plus sign. As the bread bakes, the cuts will spread apart.

5. Bake for about 40 minutes, or until the loaves are golden brown. Cool thoroughly on a wire rack before slicing.

FRUIT AND HONEY LOAF

A sweet, cake-like loaf filled with things that are both good and good for you.
Enjoy a slice with afternoon tea, or with a good cup of coffee any time.

1. Preheat the oven to 300°F. Butter a 9-x-5-inch bread pan and set aside.

2. Place the honey and butter in a large mixing bowl and stir with a wooden spoon. Add the salt, egg, and buttermilk, and beat with the spoon until well blended. Add the remaining ingredients and stir just long enough to moisten the dry ingredients—do not overstir.

3. Pour the batter into the prepared pan and bake for 1 hour and 40 minutes, or until a toothpick inserted in the center comes out clean. The loaf will be very brown and begin to shrink away from the sides of the pan. Cool on a wire rack for 30 minutes, then turn the loaf out of the pan. Finish cooling the bread on the rack before serving.

YIELD: 1 LARGE LOAF

1 cup honey

2 tablespoons soft butter

1 teaspoon salt

1 egg

¾ cup buttermilk*

2½ cups whole wheat flour

¼ cup bran or wheat germ

⅓ cup raisins

⅓ cup currants

1 tablespoon grated
orange peel

1 teaspoon baking soda

* As a substitute, you can use plain yogurt.

DATE NUT BREAD

Another sweet, wholesome quick bread. Try a slice with cream cheese.

YIELD:
2 MEDIUM LOAVES

1½ cups chopped dates
  (8-ounce package)

½ cup raisins

2 cups boiling water

2 eggs

¾ cup brown sugar

2 teaspoons baking powder

1 teaspoon baking soda

1 teaspoon vanilla extract

2 cups whole wheat flour

2 cups bran (miller's bran,
  not bran cereal)

1 cup chopped walnuts
  or pecans

1. Preheat the oven to 350°F. Butter two 8-x-4-inch bread pans and set aside. Place the dates and raisins in a small bowl, add the boiling water, and set aside to cool.

2. Place the eggs, brown sugar, baking powder, baking soda, and vanilla in a large mixing bowl and stir with a wooden spoon. Stir in the flour, bran, and nuts. Add the cooled dates, raisins, and their liquid, and stir (do not beat) just until the ingredients are mixed—do not overstir.

3. Divide the batter into the prepared pans and bake for 45 minutes, or until a toothpick inserted into the center of a loaf comes out clean. Cool on a wire rack for 30 minutes, then turn the loaves out of the pans. Finish cooling the bread on the rack before serving.

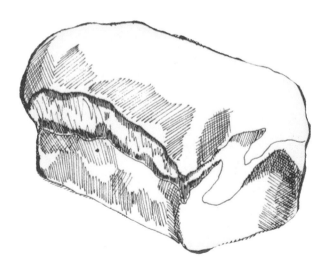

CRANBERRY NUT BREAD

This moist, rich, slightly sweet fruit bread makes an appropriate (and delicious) small gift at Thanksgiving or the end-of-year holidays. If you are using frozen cranberries, do not thaw them before chopping. This bread will keep for days in the refrigerator and freezes very well.

1. Preheat the oven to 350°F. Butter two 8-x-4-inch bread pans and set aside.

2. Place the egg, orange juice, oil, sugar, cranberries, and orange peel in a large mixing bowl and stir with a wooden spoon. Add the flour, walnuts, salt, baking powder, and baking soda, and stir (do not beat) just until the ingredients are mixed—do not overstir.

3. Divide the batter into the prepared pans and bake for about 1 hour, or until a toothpick inserted into the center of a loaf comes out clean. Cool on a wire rack for 30 minutes, then turn the loaves out of the pans. Finish cooling the bread on the rack before serving.

YIELD: 2 MEDIUM LOAVES

1 egg

$3/4$ cup orange juice

$1/4$ cup oil

1 cup sugar

2 cups coarsely chopped fresh or frozen cranberries

1 tablespoon grated orange peel

2 cups whole wheat flour

$1/2$ cup chopped walnuts

1 teaspoon salt

$1 1/2$ teaspoons baking powder

$1/2$ teaspoon baking soda

CARROT BREAD

This rich dessert bread is sweet and spicy. Like most quick breads, it keeps well for several days in the refrigerator, and several months in the freezer. Kids love to eat their carrots this way. Enjoy plain or topped with a spread of cream cheese.

YIELD: 2 LARGE LOAVES

4 eggs

1½ cups sugar

1¼ cups oil

2 cups finely shredded raw carrots

3 cups whole wheat flour

2 teaspoons baking powder

1½ teaspoons baking soda

2 teaspoons cinnamon

¼ teaspoon salt

1. Preheat the oven to 350°F. Butter two 9-x-5-inch bread pans and set aside.

2. Place the eggs, sugar, and oil in a mixing bowl and beat with a wooden spoon. Add all the remaining ingredients and stir until well blended.

3. Divide the batter into the prepared pans and bake for 1 hour, or until a toothpick inserted into the center of a loaf comes out clean. Cool on a wire rack for 30 minutes, then turn the loaves out of the pans. Finish cooling the bread on the rack before serving.

VARIATION

Carrot-Nut Bread Add 1 cup coarsely chopped walnuts to the batter.

ZUCCHINI BREAD

Zucchini has always been a bumper crop in our garden. Even after everyone groans at the thought of zucchini as a vegetable again, they always love zucchini bread.

1. Preheat the oven to 350°F. Butter two 9-x-5-inch bread pans and set aside.

2. Place the eggs, sugar, oil, and vanilla extract in a mixing bowl and beat with a wooden spoon. Add all the remaining ingredients and stir until well blended.

3. Divide the batter into the prepared pans and bake for 1 hour, or until a toothpick inserted into the center of a loaf comes out clean. Cool on a wire rack for 30 minutes, then turn the loaves out of the pans. Finish cooling the bread on the rack before serving.

YIELD:
2 LARGE LOAVES

4 eggs

1½ cups sugar

1¼ cups oil

1 teaspoon vanilla extract

2 cups finely shredded raw zucchini

3 cups whole wheat flour

2 teaspoons baking powder

1½ teaspoons baking soda

1 tablespoon cinnamon

¼ teaspoon salt

PUMPKIN BREAD

This is one of the best of all fruit breads—really a cake in bread's clothing. Served with a dollop of whipped cream, it makes an appropriate finale to a Thanksgiving dinner and a change from the ubiquitous pie. You can safely make it weeks ahead of time and keep it in the freezer. Use a fresh pumpkin if it's that time of year and you happen to have one. If not, canned pumpkin does the job perfectly and certainly saves time and trouble.

YIELD: 2 LARGE LOAVES

3 cups cooked, mashed pumpkin (or 29-ounce can)

1 cup oil

1 cup honey

1 cup brown sugar

1 cup chopped walnuts

1 teaspoon salt

1 teaspoon ground cloves

1 teaspoon cinnamon

4 teaspoons baking soda

2 cups unbleached white flour

2½ cups whole wheat flour

½ cup wheat germ

1. Preheat the oven to 350°F. Butter two 9-x-5-inch bread pans and set aside.

2. Place the pumpkin, oil, honey, and brown sugar in a large mixing bowl and stir with a wooden spoon. Add all the remaining ingredients and stir until well blended.

3. Divide the batter into the prepared pans and bake for 1 hour, or until a toothpick inserted into the center of a loaf comes out clean. Cool on a wire rack for 30 minutes, then turn the loaves out of the pans. Finish cooling the bread on the rack before serving.

DOWN-HOME BISCUITS

The only secret to turning out light and flaky biscuits is to handle the dough as little as possible. Many cooks have made great reputations on their biscuits, but it's hard to understand why; biscuits are extremely easy to make and take very little time.

1. Preheat the oven to 450°F.

2. Sift the flour, baking powder, and salt in a large mixing bowl. Add the butter and work it in with your fingertips until the mixture is crumbly and even in texture. Add the milk and knead the dough *very lightly* (about 20 strokes)—just to make it smooth.

3. Place the dough on a lightly floured board. Dust a little flour on your hands and gently flatten the dough to a $3/4$-inch thickness. Using a floured 3-inch biscuit cutter or rim of a glass, cut circles from the dough and place on an unoiled baking sheet, leaving enough room between them to allow for expansion. (You can cut the dough into squares or diamonds if you prefer.)

4. Place in the oven and bake for 12 to 15 minutes, or until the biscuits are golden brown. Serve hot from the oven.

YIELD: ABOUT 12 BISCUITS

2 cups unbleached white flour

1 tablespoon baking powder

1 teaspoon salt

4 tablespoons soft butter

$3/4$ cup cold milk

VARIATIONS

Cheese Biscuits Add $1/2$ cup grated Cheddar (or other) cheese when adding the milk.

Herb Biscuits Add $1/4$ teaspoon each of dried oregano, chives, and basil to the dough along with the dry ingredients. Or, if you prefer, add $3/4$ teaspoon of a single herb, such as dill weed. If you use fresh herbs, double the quantity.

BASIC MUFFINS

A batch of muffins can always be whipped up quickly. Well-made muffins are tender and light with nicely rounded tops. They also have a fine texture with no big air tunnels running through them. For best results, put all the dry ingredients into the bowl first (including any nuts, fruits, or the like) and then add the liquid. Stir no more than about a dozen times, leaving the batter lumpy. Although several variations are given for this basic recipe, you can undoubtedly think up many more on your own.

YIELD: 12 TO 15 MUFFINS

2 cups unbleached white flour

1 tablespoon baking powder

$1/2$ teaspoon salt

4–6 tablespoons sugar, depending on desired sweetness

1 egg, slightly beaten

4 tablespoons melted butter

1 cup milk

1 tablespoon sugar plus $1/2$ teaspoon cinnamon for topping (optional)

1. Preheat the oven to 400°F. Grease a standard muffin tin or line with paper baking cups, and set aside.

2. Sift the flour, baking powder, and salt into a bowl. Stir in the sugar, then add the egg, butter, and milk. Stir *just* enough to moisten the dry ingredients (it will be lumpy)—do not overstir.

3. Spoon the batter into the prepared muffin cups. Fill each cup about two-thirds. Sprinkle with cinnamon-sugar mixture, if using.

4. Bake about 20 minutes, or until the muffins are brown and a toothpick inserted into the center comes out clean. Cool on a wire rack for at least 10 minutes before removing the muffins from the tin.

VARIATIONS

Blueberry Muffins Add 1 cup blueberries (rinsed and patted dry) to the flour mixture.

Dried Fruit Muffins Add $1/2$ cup chopped dates, prunes, apricots, raisins, figs, or other dried fruit to the flour mixture.

TIP If you have a lever-type ice cream scoop, use it to fill your muffin pans.

Nut Muffins Add $\frac{1}{2}$ cup unsalted chopped nuts to the flour mixture.

Chocolate Muffins Use 6 tablespoons sugar, and mix 3 ounces melted semi-sweet chocolate with the melted butter.

Chocolate Chocolate Chip Muffins Add $\frac{1}{2}$ cup mini chocolate chips to the Chocolate Muffins variation (above).

Whole Wheat Muffins Substitute 1 cup whole wheat flour for an equivalent amount of white flour.

Bran Muffins Substitute 1 cup bran (miller's bran, not bran cereal) for an equivalent amount of flour.

> **TIP** Before you begin preparing a batch of muffins, be sure the oven is hot and the pan greased (or lined with fluted muffin papers). This way, you can get your muffin batter into the oven immediately.

CORN MUFFINS

A perennial favorite. Feel free to gild the lily by adding a cupful of rinsed and dried blueberries.

1. Preheat the oven to 400°F. Grease a standard muffin tin or line with paper baking cups, and set aside.

2. Sift the flour, sugar, baking powder, salt, and cornmeal in a large mixing bowl and stir with a wooden spoon until blended. Add the milk, eggs, and butter, and stir with the spoon *just* enough to moisten the dry ingredients (it will be lumpy)—do not overstir.

3. Spoon the batter into the prepared muffin cups. Fill each cup about two-thirds.

4. Bake for about 20 minutes, or until a toothpick inserted in the center of a muffin comes out clean. Cool on a wire rack at least 10 minutes before removing the muffins from the tin.

YIELD: 12 TO 15 MUFFINS

1 cup unbleached white flour

$\frac{1}{4}$ cup sugar

4 teaspoons baking powder

$\frac{3}{4}$ teaspoon salt

1 cup yellow cornmeal

1 cup milk

2 eggs

4 tablespoons ($\frac{1}{2}$ stick) soft butter

SCONES

Scones, warm from the oven and served with plenty of butter, whipped or clotted cream, and a pot of strawberry preserves, are the very heart of an English Cream Tea.

YIELD: 12 SCONES

2 cups unbleached flour

2 tablespoons sugar

1 teaspoon baking powder

$^3/_4$ cup (1$^1/_2$ sticks) cold butter, cut into 1-inch slices

2 eggs, lightly beaten

$^3/_4$ cup heavy cream

$^1/_2$ cup raisins or dried currants

1 egg yolk plus 1 tablespoon heavy cream

3 tablespoons sugar for topping

1. Preheat the oven to 350°F. Lightly butter a large baking sheet and set aside.

2. Place the flour, sugar, and baking powder in a large mixing bowl. Add the butter and lightly work it in with your fingertips until the mixture is crumbly and resembles coarse meal. Add the eggs and cream, and blend in with a spoon, stirring as lightly as possible. (Remember, the less work-out you give this dough, the lighter your scones will be.) Fold in the raisins.

3. Transfer the dough to a lightly floured board and gently shape into a $^1/_2$-inch thick rectangle. Cut the dough into 6 squares, then cut the squares diagonally to make 12 triangles. Place on the prepared baking sheet, leaving enough room between them to allow for expansion.

4. In a small bowl, beat together the egg yolk and cream, then brush some on top of each scone and sprinkle with sugar. Bake for 20 to 25 minutes, or until light golden brown. Serve hot from the oven.

8. Flatbreads, Rolls, and More

This chapter begins with a variety of flatbreads, historically, the oldest type of bread. As you know, in very ancient times, all bread was unleavened, or flat. Later, the Hebrews had sourdough, and the Egyptians developed yeast; and eventually, raised bread made its way through most of Europe and parts of Asia and the New World. However, there are still many areas where the old-style flatbreads are favored and commonly served. Pita, which originated in Mesopotamia, continues to be the bread of Greece and the Middle East; lavash and pideh are popular in Armenia; poori and other flatbreads are staples in India; and matzoh is still the bread eaten by Jewish people all over the world during the eight days of Passover.

Other recipes in this chapter include breads with interesting and distinctive shapes. There is a variety of roll recipes, including a basic dinner roll that shows you how easy it is to turn the same dough into crescents, cloverleafs, and Parker House rolls, as well as fan tans and love knots. Strictly speaking, you can make good rolls with any bread dough. But from a traditional culinary point of view, rolls are usually less dense and have a more feathery crumb than most breads. The recipes in this chapter, with their tips on shaping, will enable you to make perfect examples of the roll-baker's art.

You'll also discover how easy it is to make a crisp pizza crust ready for the toppings of your choice, a fragrant Focaccia bread, chewy bagels, and those big, fat, soft pretzels that are so popular at carnivals and are a trademark of the Pennsylvania Dutch. There's even a recipe for teething biscuits for those babies you love so much.

These recipes are fun to prepare because by following just a few relatively simple steps, you can turn out highly professional looking flatbreads, rolls, and novelty breads; some of them might surprise even you.

PITA

*Pita originated in Mesopotamia and is still the common bread of the Middle East.
The small round or oval breads puff up when baked, then deflate; when they are split open,
there is a space in the center that can be stuffed with a filling. A filled pita is a meal that can be
eaten on the run. Try it with Hummus (page 135) either as a filling or a dip, or enjoy the pita plain.*

YIELD:
8 PITAS

1 tablespoon (1 packet) active dry yeast

1¼ cups lukewarm water

2 teaspoons salt

1 tablespoon oil

3–4 cups unbleached white flour

1. Place the yeast and water in a dishpan or large mixing bowl and stir with a wooden spoon. Add the salt, oil, and 3 cups of flour and continue to stir, adding more flour a little at a time, until the dough is easy to handle. Knead for 5 minutes, or until the dough is smooth and shiny. Shape into a ball.

2. Spread a little oil on the bottom and sides of the bowl. Add the ball of dough, then turn it over, oiled side up. Cover and set in a warm spot for about 50 minutes, or until the dough doubles in bulk. Lightly oil a large baking sheet and set aside.

3. Punch down the risen dough and cut in half, then cut each half into 4 equal pieces (for a total of 8). Form each piece into a ball and let rest for 10 minutes. On a floured board, roll out each ball of dough into a ¼-inch-thick circle. (Don't be concerned if your circles are irregular; the handmade look is part of their charm.)

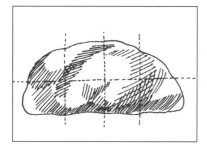

Divide the dough into
8 pieces.

Roll each piece into a ball.

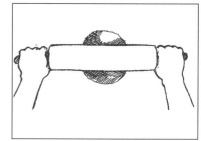

Roll out each ball of dough
into a 1/4-inch-thick circle.

4. Place the circles on the prepared baking sheet, cover with a towel, and let rise 30 to 40 minutes, or until doubled in bulk.

5. Place in a preheated 475°F oven and bake about 15 minutes, or until the pitas have just *started* to brown. Remove from the oven and cover the pitas with a clean kitchen towel (to keep them soft as they cool). They will lose their puffiness, but when you carefully split one open, you will find a pouch in the center.

TIP If you are not going to use your pitas promptly, put them in a plastic bag to keep them soft. They also freeze very well. To reheat, wrap in aluminum foil and place in a 375°F oven for 10 to 15 minutes, or until completely thawed.

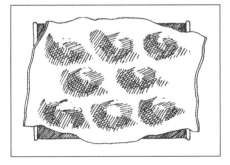

Place the circles on a baking sheet, cover, and let rise.

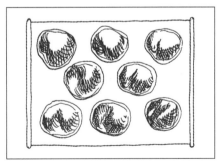

Bake until the pitas have just started to brown.

LAVASH

Lavash is a crisp Armenian flatbread that is good with any food and lends itself especially
well to dips and soft cheese. Break off pieces of the crisp bread and pile them into a basket.
Soft lavash is also good as wrap-around bread for such fillings as hummus, cheese, and kebabs.
To soften, hold the lavash briefly under running water to wet both sides.
Shake off the water, then wrap in a towel for a half hour or so.

YIELD:
4 LAVASH

1 tablespoon (1 packet)
   active dry yeast

1 1/4 cups lukewarm water

1/4 cup oil

2 teaspoons salt

1 teaspoon sugar

4–4 1/2 cups unbleached
   white flour

1. Place the yeast and water in a dishpan or large mixing bowl and stir with a wooden spoon. Add the oil, salt, sugar, and 2 cups of the flour, and beat with the spoon for a minute or two until well blended.

2. Add 2 more cups of flour, then squeeze the mixture with your hands until the flour disappears. If it is too wet to pick up, add a little more flour. As soon as you can handle the dough, begin to knead directly in the bowl (or on a floured board), adding more flour as necessary. Knead for about 5 minutes, or until the dough is smooth and elastic. Shape into a ball.

3. Spread a little oil on the bottom and sides of the bowl. Add the ball of dough, then turn it over, oiled side up. Cover and set in a warm place for about an hour, or until the dough doubles in bulk.

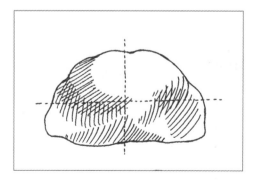

Divide the dough into fourths.

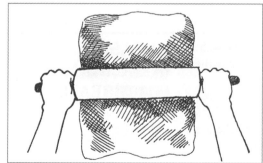

Roll out each piece into a rectangle.

4. Punch down the risen dough and cut it into 4 equal pieces. On a floured board, roll out 2 pieces into 10-x-14-inch rectangles (or 13-inch circles). Place them on two large ungreased baking sheets. Prick the top of the dough all over with a fork. (Unless you have two ovens, you will have to bake this bread in two batches. Once the first batch is baked, roll out the remaining 2 pieces of dough and repeat the steps.)

5. Place in a preheated 400°F oven and bake about 20 to 30 minutes, or until the surface of the lavash becomes bubbly and crisp, and the bottom is brown (you can peek with the help of a spatula). If the top isn't very crisp, slide the pan under the broiler for *just a few seconds.* When doing this, keep the broiler door open, the potholder handy, and *watch;* lavash can turn black in a flash.

6. Cool the lavash on a wire rack. When thoroughly cool, break into pieces and store in an airtight container, where it will keep for a few weeks.

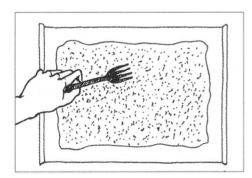

Prick the top of the dough
with a fork.

Bake until the lavash is
crisp and bubbly.

PIDEH

Pideh is an Armenian semi-flatbread. Unlike lavash, it is soft, not cracker-like, and milk and butter make it richer than most flatbreads. It is good to serve with meals and is particularly appropriate with such specialties as shish kebab or any other fine Armenian-style dishes.

**YIELD:
2 PIDEH**

4–4½ cups unbleached white flour

2 teaspoons salt

1½ tablespoons sugar

1 cup warm milk

2 tablespoons melted butter

1 tablespoon (1 packet) active dry yeast

½ cup lukewarm water

2 tablespoons melted butter for brushing on loaves

1 tablespoon sesame seeds for topping

1. Place the flour, salt, and sugar in a dishpan or large mixing bowl. Make a well in the center and pour in the milk, butter, yeast, and water. Mix it all together with your fingers, adding more flour a little at a time, until the dough is easy to handle. Knead for about 5 minutes, or until the dough is smooth and elastic. Shape into a ball.

2. Spread a little oil on the bottom and sides of the bowl. Add the ball of dough, then turn it over, oiled side up. Cover and set in a warm spot for an hour or more, until the dough doubles in bulk.

3. Punch down the risen dough and knead for a minute or so. Cover and set in a warm spot for an hour, or until the dough doubles in bulk a second time. Butter two 9- or 10-inch round cake pans and set aside.

4. After the second rising, punch down the dough and cut in half with a knife. Roll each half into a ball. On a floured board, roll out each ball into an 8-inch circle about 1 inch thick. Place in the prepared pans, brush the tops with melted butter, and sprinkle with sesame seeds. Let rise another 30 to 40 minutes, or until doubled in bulk.

5. Place in a preheated 375°F oven and bake about 40 to 45 minutes, or until the bread is golden brown. Cool on a wire rack before serving.

MATZOH

*The Bible never gets around to saying what **kind** of bread the ancient Hebrews had to bake in such a hurry when they fled from Egypt, but it's safe to assume that they had neither white flour nor machinery for making perfect squares. Their unleavened bread—matzoh— **might** have been something like the one made from this recipe. It is light and crisp, yet strong enough to hold your favorite dips and spreads.*

1. Preheat the oven to 375°F. Lightly sprinkle a large baking sheet with flour and set aside.

2. Place the water in a large mixing bowl, then add 2 cups of the flour, the oil, and salt. Mix the ingredients first with a wooden spoon, then with your hand. Knead the dough for a minute just to see if it is firm enough to handle. If it isn't, add a little more flour. Shape the dough into a ball.

3. Cut the dough in half. On a floured board, roll out each half into a large thin circle. Place the circles on the prepared baking sheet.

4. Bake for about 40 minutes, or until the matzoh is very dry and crisp, and just beginning to brown. Remove the pan from the oven and set on a wire rack. When the matzoh is thoroughly cool, break into pieces and store in an airtight container.

**YIELD:
2 LARGE SHEETS**

1 cup water

2–2½ cups whole wheat flour

2 tablespoons oil

1 teaspoon salt

FOCACCIA

Focaccia is similar to a thick bready pizza and just as versatile. In this recipe, it is topped with rosemary, but feel free to use any topping you like. Fresh or sun-dried tomatoes, roasted vegetables, fresh or dried herbs, crumbled goat cheese, grated Parmigiano Reggiano, and sliced Greek olives are just a few delicious options. Depending on the topping, you can enjoy Focaccia as a dinner bread or lunch entrée. You can also cut it into bite-sized pieces and serve as a delicious appetizer.

YIELD:
2 MEDIUM ROUNDS

2 teaspoons active dry yeast

$\frac{1}{4}$ cup lukewarm water

1 tablespoon salt

3$\frac{3}{4}$–4 cups unbleached white flour

1$\frac{1}{4}$ cup plus 1 tablespoon lukewarm water

TOPPING

$\frac{1}{4}$ cup extra-virgin olive oil

2 teaspoons coarse sea salt

2 teaspoons finely chopped fresh rosemary, or 1 teaspoon dried (or to taste)

1. Place the yeast and $\frac{1}{4}$ cup water in a dishpan or large bowl, stir with a wooden spoon, and let sit for 5 minutes. Add the salt, 3 $\frac{3}{4}$ cups of flour, and the additional water. Stir as long as you can, then mix with your hands, adding a small amount of extra flour if the dough is too wet to pick up (just keep in mind that the wetter the dough, the airier the Focaccia will be). Knead for about 5 minutes, or until the dough is smooth and elastic. Shape into a ball.

2. Spread a little oil on the bottom and sides of the bowl. Add the ball of dough, then turn it over, oiled side up. Cover and set in a warm spot for 1 to 2 hours, or until the dough doubles in bulk. Lightly oil two 9-inch round cake pans and set aside.

3. Punch down the risen dough, cut in half, and place in the prepared pans. Gently stretch the dough to fit the pans. (If the dough resists, let it rest 5 or 10 minutes, then try again.) Cover and let rise about 30 to 40 minutes, or until doubled in bulk.

4. With your fingers, make dimples all over the surface of the risen dough. Drizzle with olive oil, and sprinkle with salt and rosemary.

5. Place in a preheated 450°F oven and bake for 15 to 18 minutes, or until the Focaccia is golden brown. Cool on a wire rack. Serve warm or at room temperature.

PIZZA CRUST

Everybody loves pizza. This easy recipe will make crusts for two large pies. You can use the dough right away, or store it for later use. Simply place it in a plastic bag that has been lightly dusted with flour and refrigerate for up to three days. Even refrigerated, the dough will rise somewhat, so be sure to leave space in the bag. When ready to use, remove the dough from the refrigerator and let it come to room temperature (about 20 minutes).

YIELD: 2 LARGE CRUSTS

1 tablespoon (1 packet) active dry yeast

$\frac{1}{4}$ cup lukewarm water

1 teaspoon sugar

1 cup lukewarm water

1 tablespoon olive oil

1 teaspoon salt

$3\frac{1}{2}$–$4\frac{1}{2}$ cups unbleached white flour

1. Place the yeast, $\frac{1}{4}$ cup lukewarm water, and sugar in a dishpan or large bowl. Stir with a wooden spoon to dissolve the yeast. Add 1 cup lukewarm water, the olive oil, salt, and $3\frac{1}{2}$ cups flour. Stir the ingredients, adding more flour a little at a time, until the dough is easy to handle.

2. Knead the dough directly in the bowl (or on a floured board), adding more flour as necessary. Knead about 10 minutes, or until the dough is smooth, elastic, and very easy to handle. Shape into a ball.

3. Spread a little oil on the bottom and sides of the bowl. Add the ball of dough, then turn it over, oiled side up. Cover and set in a warm spot for about an hour, or until the dough doubles in bulk. Lightly sprinkle two 12-inch-round pizza pans with cornmeal and set aside. (You can also make a large rectangular pizza, using an 18-x-13-inch sheet pan instead.)

4. Punch down the risen dough, cut in half, and form each half into a ball. On a floured board, pat or roll out each ball of dough into a circle. Place the circle over your floured knuckles and gently stretch to just about the size of the pan.

5. Place the rounds on the prepared pans and flatten the center with your hands, leaving a raised edge around the rim.

6. Add your topping of choice, then place in a preheated 500°F oven and bake about 10 to 15 minutes, or until the crust is golden brown.

DINNER ROLLS

*For dinner rolls that are light, tender, and delicious, try this single
all-purpose recipe. It includes instructions for shaping the dough into pan rolls,
love knots, cloverleaf rolls, fan tans, crescent rolls, and Parker House rolls.*

YIELD: Varies based on shape of rolls

3/4 cup lukewarm water

1 tablespoon (1 packet)
  active dry yeast

3 tablespoons sugar

1/2 cup mashed potatoes,
  at room temperature
  (see TIP on page 63)

5 tablespoons butter,
  at room temperature

1 egg

2 tablespoons nonfat dry milk
  powder

1 teaspoon salt

3–4 cups unbleached white flour

3 tablespoons melted butter for
  brushing on baked rolls

1. Place the water, yeast, and sugar in a dishpan or large bowl and stir with a wooden spoon. Stir in the potatoes, butter, egg, milk powder, and salt. Add 2 cups of flour and beat with the spoon until well blended.

2. Add 1 more cup of flour, then squeeze the mixture with your hands until the flour disappears. If it is too wet to pick up, add a little more flour. As soon as you can handle the dough, sprinkle with a bit more flour and begin to knead directly in the bowl (or on a floured board), adding more flour as necessary. Knead for 5 to 7 minutes, or until the dough feels smooth and elastic. Shape into a ball.

3. Spread a little oil on the bottom and sides of the bowl. Add the ball of dough, then turn it over, oiled side up. Cover and set in a warm spot for an hour, or until the dough doubles in bulk.

4. Punch down the risen dough, which is now ready to be formed into rolls. Choose one of the shapes beginning on the next page, and follow the instructions. After forming the rolls, cover and let rise about 30 minutes, or until doubled in bulk.

5. Place in a preheated 400°F oven and bake about 20 minutes, or until the rolls have reached the desired shade of brown. Place on a wire rack and brush the tops with melted butter to keep them soft. Serve warm or at room temperature.

SHAPE VARIATIONS

Pan Rolls Butter two 9-inch round cake pans and set aside. Cut the dough in half and roll each piece with your hands to form a rope about a foot long. Cut each rope into 12 equal pieces for a total of 24. Roll each piece into a ball and arrange 12 balls in each prepared pan (it doesn't matter if they are touching; once baked, they will all be joined together).

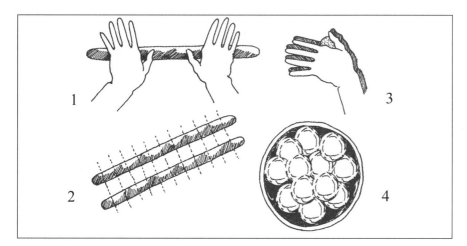

Yield: 24

1. Roll the dough into two 12-inch ropes.
2. Cut each rope into 12 pieces.
3. Roll the pieces into balls.
4. Place the balls in round cake pans.

Cloverleaf Rolls Butter a 12-cup muffin tin and set aside. Cut the dough in half and roll each piece with your hands to form a rope about 18 inches long. Cut each rope into 18 equal pieces. Roll each piece into a small ball. Place 3 balls in each muffin cup.

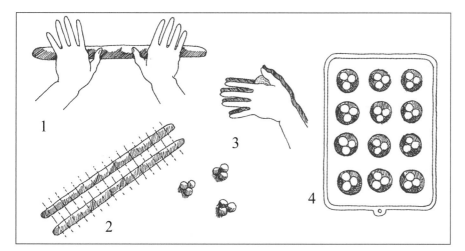

Yield: 12

1. Roll the dough into two 18-inch ropes.
2. Cut each rope into 18 pieces.
3. Roll the pieces into balls.
4. Place 3 balls in each muffin cup.

Crescent Rolls Butter a large baking sheet and set aside. Cut the dough in half. Using a rolling pin, roll out each piece into a circle about 8 inches in diameter. With a sharp knife, cut the circle into 4 equal quarters, then make two diagonal cuts to form 8 equal wedges. Starting at the curved outside edge, roll up each wedge until the point is rolled just over the top. Curve each roll into a crescent shape, and place them point-side up on the prepared baking sheet, leaving enough space between them to allow for expansion.

Yield: 16

1. Cut the dough in half.

2. Roll out each half into 8-inch circles, and cut into 8 wedges.

3. Roll up each wedge.

4. Place on a baking sheet point side up.

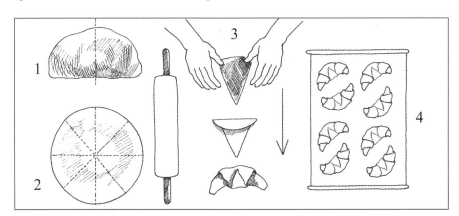

Parker House Rolls Butter a large baking sheet and set aside. Cut the dough in half. Using a rolling pin, roll out each piece into a 3/8-inch thick rectangle. With a floured 3-inch biscuit cutter or rim of a glass, cut circles from each rectangle, then piece the scraps together to cut more. Brush each with a little melted butter and fold them over—not quite in half (the top of the roll should cover only two-thirds of the bottom). Gently press the edges together. Place on the prepared baking sheet, leaving enough room between them to allow for expansion.

Yield: About 16

1. Cut 3-inch circles from the dough.

2. Fold each circle not quite in half.

3. Place on a baking sheet.

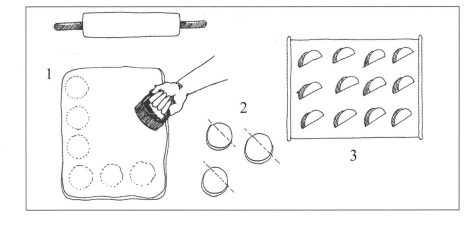

Fan Tans Butter two 12-cup muffin tins and set aside. Cut the dough in half. Using a rolling pin, roll out each piece into a rectangle about 8-x-16 inches. Brush with melted butter. Cut each rectangle lengthwise into five equal strips. Stack the strips, then cut the stack crosswise into 12 equal pieces. Carefully pick up each little stack and place in the muffin cups, cut edges up.

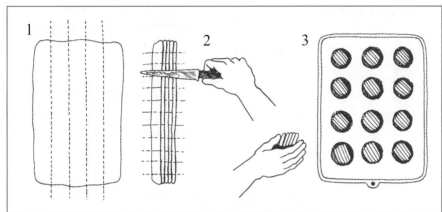

Yield: 24

1. Cut the dough lengthwise into 5 equal strips.
2. Stack the strips and cut crosswise into 12 equal pieces.
3. Place each stack cut side up in a muffin cup.

Love Knots Butter a large baking sheet and set aside. Cut the dough in half and roll each piece with your hands to form a rope about 36 inches (3 feet) long. Cut each rope into 6 pieces (about 6 inches long) for a total of 12. Tie each piece in a single overhand knot and tuck the ends under. Place the knots on the prepared baking sheet, leaving enough space between them to allow for expansion.

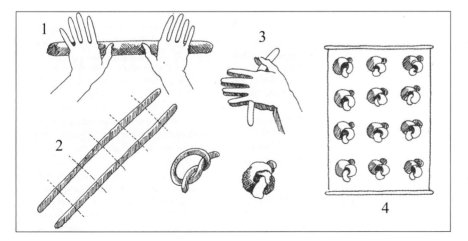

Yield: 12

1. Roll the dough into two 36-inch ropes.
2. Cut each rope into six 6-inch pieces.
3. Tie each piece in a knot and tuck the ends under.
4. Place the knots on a baking sheet.

FRENCH-STYLE HARD ROLLS

Lovely continental-style rolls—hard and crusty on the outside, light and airy on the inside. Make them round or rectangular.

YIELD: 12 ROLLS

1½ cups lukewarm water

1 tablespoon (1 packet) active dry yeast

2 teaspoons salt

3–4 cups unbleached white flour

1–2 tablespoons cornmeal for the baking sheet

1 egg white plus 1 tablespoon cold water

1. Place the water, yeast, and salt in dishpan or large mixing bowl and stir with a wooden spoon. Add 3 cups of flour and continue to stir, adding more flour, a little at a time, until you can handle the dough. Begin to knead directly in the bowl (or on a floured board), adding more flour as necessary. Knead for about 5 minutes, or until the dough feels smooth and elastic. Shape into a ball.

2. Spread a little softened butter on the bottom and sides of the bowl. Add the ball of dough, then turn it over, buttered side up. Cover and set in a warm spot for about an hour, or until the dough doubles in bulk. Punch down the risen dough, cover, and let rise a second time for about 45 minutes, or until doubled in bulk again. Lightly sprinkle a large baking sheet with cornmeal and set aside.

3. Punch down the risen dough again and knead for a minute or so. Cut in half and roll the dough with your hands to form two ropes, each about 18 inches long. Cut each rope into 6 equal pieces. Shape the pieces into balls or rectangles (or both), and place on the prepared baking sheet, leaving enough room between them to allow for expansion.

4. In a small bowl, beat together the egg white and cold water, then brush some on the rolls. Cover with a clean dishtowel that has been dipped in cold water and tightly wrung out. Let the rolls rise about 50 minutes, or until doubled in bulk, then brush again with the egg wash.

5. Place in a preheated 375°F oven, and set a pan of very hot water on the bottom rack (to create steam as the rolls bake). After the first 15 minutes of baking, brush the rolls once again with the egg wash, then continue to bake another 15 minutes, or until golden brown. Cool slightly on a wire rack before serving.

WHOLE WHEAT ROLLS

These rolls don't rise as high as white rolls, but they have a good wheaty taste and a fine chewy texture. You can shape them as described or divide each one into three pencil-thick ropes and braid them. This dough requires only one rising (just before the rolls are baked). For a less chewy, finer-textured roll, let the dough rise twice— once before shaping the rolls, then again before baking.

1. Place the yeast, water, salt, oil, and 4 cups of flour in a dishpan or large mixing bowl, and mix together with your hands. If the dough is too wet to pick up, add a little more flour. As soon as you can handle the dough, begin to knead directly in the bowl (or on a floured board), adding more flour as necessary. Knead for 5 minutes or until the dough is very elastic, then shape into a ball. Lightly grease a large baking sheet and set aside.

2. Cut the dough in half, then divide each half into 6 equal pieces (for a total of 12). Roll each piece into a ball, then flatten the balls with your hand to a 1-inch thickness. With a sharp pointy knife that has been dipped in flour, make five deep cuts into each roll that extend outward from the center (like flower petals). Begin the cuts about a quarter inch from the center—the uncut area in the very center of the roll should be about the size of a dime.

3. Transfer the rolls to the prepared baking sheet, leaving enough space between them to allow for expansion. Brush with the softened butter, cover, and let rise for about an hour, or until doubled in bulk.

4. Place in a 350°F oven and bake for 25 to 30 minutes, or until the rolls are quite brown on the bottom. Cool on a wire rack. Serve warm or at room temperature.

YIELD: 12 ROLLS

1 tablespoon (1 packet) active dry yeast

1½ cups lukewarm water

1 teaspoon salt

2 tablespoons oil

4–5 cups whole wheat flour

2–3 tablespoons soft butter or oil

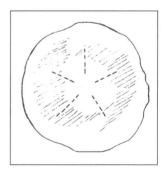

In each roll, make five deep cuts that extend outward from the center.

NEW YORK BAGELS

Delicious plain or topped with butter or cream cheese, doughnut-shaped bagels are chewy and satisfying. Serve them warm, fresh from the oven; split and toasted; or buttered and broiled for a minute. You can make a big batch because they freeze perfectly. In New York City, where bagels are practically a staple, "a bagel with a schmear" is Newyorkese for a bagel with cream cheese.

YIELD:
12 BAGELS

1 tablespoon (1 packet) active dry yeast

1½ cups lukewarm water

1 tablespoon sugar

1 tablespoon oil

1 tablespoon salt

4½–5½ cups unbleached white flour

Sesame or poppy seeds for sprinkling on top (optional)

FOR THE COOKING WATER

1 tablespoon sugar

1 teaspoon salt

1. Place the yeast, water, sugar, oil, salt, and 4 cups of flour in a large mixing bowl and mix together with your hands. If the dough is too wet to pick up, add a little more flour. As soon as you can handle the dough, knead it for about 10 minutes, or until smooth and elastic. Shape into a ball.

2. Spread a little oil on the bottom and sides of the bowl. Add the ball of dough, then turn it over, oiled-side up. Cover and set in a warm spot for about an hour, or until the dough doubles in bulk. Lightly sprinkle a sheet of parchment paper or clean kitchen towel with flour and set aside. Also grease a large baking sheet and set aside.

3. Punch down the risen dough and cut in half. Divide each half into 6 equal pieces (for a total of 12). Dust your hands with a little flour and roll each piece of dough into a 10-inch-long rope. Join the ends and pinch together to form a smooth circle; if necessary, use a drop of water to make a good seal.

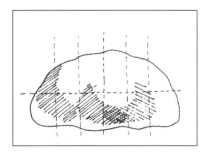

Divide the dough into 12 equal pieces.

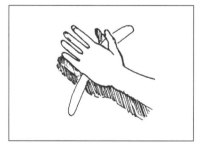

Roll each piece into a 10-inch rope.

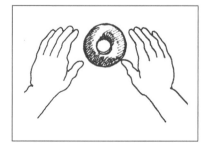

Join the ends and pinch together.

4. Transfer the bagels to the floured parchment paper or towel, cover, and let rise for 20 minutes. While they are rising, fill your largest-diameter pot halfway with water. Add 1 tablespoon sugar and 1 teaspoon salt and bring to a boil. Reduce the heat so the water boils gently.

5. Lift each risen bagel with a spatula and carefully slide it into the boiling water without crowding the pot. (You will have to do this in several batches.) Boil the bagels on one side for 3 minutes, then turn over and boil another 3 minutes. Remove from the pot and place on paper towels to drain for a minute or so. Sprinkle with seeds (if using).

6. Transfer the bagels to the greased baking sheet. (If they don't all fit without crowding, put the overflow on a greased cake pan.) Place in a preheated 400°F oven and bake for 20 to 25 minutes, or until rich golden brown. Cool on a wire rack. Serve warm or at room temperature.

Lift the risen bagels
with a spatula, and . . .

slide them into a
pot of boiling water.

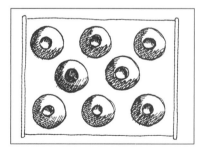

Place on a baking sheet.

EGG BAGELS

Egg bagels are a richer, less chewy model than the regular variety.

1 tablespoon (1 packet)
active dry yeast

1$\frac{1}{4}$ cups lukewarm water

2 eggs, lightly beaten

2 tablespoons oil

2 teaspoons salt

1 tablespoon sugar

4$\frac{1}{2}$–5$\frac{1}{2}$ cups flour

1 egg plus 1 tablespoon
cold water

2 tablespoons sesame seeds
(optional)

FOR THE COOKING WATER

1 tablespoon sugar

1 teaspoon salt

1. Place the yeast, water, beaten eggs, oil, salt, sugar, and 4 cups of flour in a large mixing bowl and mix together with your hands. If the dough is too wet to pick up, add a little more flour. As soon as you can handle the dough, knead it for about 10 minutes, or until smooth and elastic. Shape into a ball.

2. Spread a little oil on the bottom and sides of the bowl. Add the ball of dough, then turn it over, oiled-side up. Cover and set in a warm spot for about an hour, or until the dough doubles in bulk. Lightly sprinkle a sheet of parchment paper or clean kitchen towel with flour and set aside. Also grease a large baking sheet and set aside.

3. Punch down the risen dough and cut into 12 equal pieces. Dust your hands with a little flour and roll each piece of dough into a 10-inch-long rope. Join the ends and pinch together to form a smooth circle; if necessary, use a drop of water to make a good seal.

4. Transfer the bagels to the floured parchment paper or towel, cover, and let rise for 20 minutes. While they are rising, fill your largest-diameter pot halfway with water. Add 1 tablespoon sugar and 1 teaspoon salt and bring to a boil. Reduce the heat so the water boils gently.

5. Lift each risen bagel with a spatula and carefully slide into the boiling water without crowding the pot. (You will have to do this in several batches.) Boil the bagels on one side for 2 minutes, then turn over and boil another 2 minutes. Remove from the pot and place on paper towels to drain for a minute or so.

6. Transfer the bagels to the greased baking sheet. (If they don't all fit without crowding, put the overflow on a greased cake pan.) In a small bowl, beat together the egg and water, then brush some on each bagel. Sprinkle with sesame seeds (if using). Place in a preheated 400°F oven and bake for about 20 minutes, or until golden brown. Cool on a wire rack. Serve warm or at room temperature.

TEETHING BISCUITS

A wholesome, nutritious treat for the baby who has everything (except his or her teeth).
Tailor the biscuits to the size of the hand that will hold them.

1. Preheat the oven to 350°F. Lightly grease a large baking sheet and set aside.

2. Place all of the ingredients in a large mixing bowl and mix with your hands. The mixture should have the consistency of clay. If it is too crumbly to stick together, add a few drops of water; if too sticky, add a little more flour.

3. Take marble-sized pinches of dough and roll into finger-size biscuits. Leave rounded or flatten a bit. Arrange the biscuits on the prepared baking sheet.

4. Bake for about 15 minutes, or until the biscuits are very hard and just beginning to color. Cool on a wire rack. When completely cooled, store the biscuits in an airtight container.

**YIELD:
2 TO 3 DOZEN**

1 cup whole wheat flour

2 tablespoons nonfat dry milk powder

2 tablespoons sugar

2 tablespoons oil

1 egg yolk

1 tablespoon water

SOFT PRETZELS

When I was a child, I often bought one of these big, fat, soft pretzels from an ancient-looking man who sold them at the schoolyard gate for 5 cents. He spread them with bright yellow mustard (from an old tin can with a wooden paddle) for a tantalizing treat. If you've never had a soft pretzel with mustard, be sure to give it a try!

YIELD:
12 PRETZELS

1 tablespoon (1 packet)
  active dry yeast

1 teaspoon sugar

1 teaspoon salt

1½ cups lukewarm water

3–4 cups unbleached
  white flour

1 egg plus
  1 teaspoon cold water

Coarse sea salt for sprinkling
  on top

1. Place the yeast, sugar, salt, and water in a large mixing bowl and stir with a wooden spoon. Add 2 cups of flour and beat with the spoon until well blended. Add more flour a little at a time until you can easily handle the dough. Knead for 5 minutes, or until the dough feels smooth and elastic. Shape into a ball.

2. Spread a little oil on the bottom and sides of the bowl. Add the ball of dough, then turn it over, oiled side up. Cover and set in a warm spot for an hour or more, or until the dough doubles in bulk. Lightly grease a large baking sheet and set aside.

3. Punch down the risen dough and cut into 12 equal pieces. (If you like extra-fat pretzels, cut 10 pieces.) Roll each piece into a rope about 16 to18 inches long and twist it into a pretzel shape.

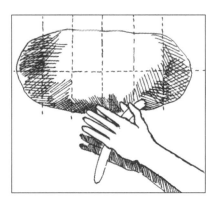

Divide the dough into
12 equal pieces, and roll each
piece into a 16 to 18-inch rope.

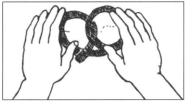

Form each rope into
a pretzel shape.

TIP If you have to bake these pretzels in several batches, it is perfectly fine to do so—the short extra rising time won't do them any harm.

A traditional twist is shown in the illustration below. You can also simply tie the rope into a loose overhand knot to form two circles, then pinch the loose ends together.

4. Place the pretzels on the prepared baking sheet, leaving enough room between them to allow for expansion. Cover and let rise for 20 minutes.

5. In a small bowl, beat together the egg and water, brush some on each pretzel, and sprinkle with coarse salt. Place in a preheated 425°F oven and bake for 15 to 20 minutes, or until the pretzels are the desired shade of golden brown. Cool on a wire rack before serving warm or at room temperature. When completely cooled, store the pretzels an airtight container.

TIP Before twisting your pretzels into shape, practice on a piece of string! When forming the actual dough, dust your hands lightly with flour to make the job simpler.

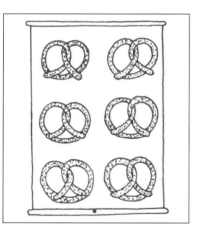

Place the pretzels
on a baking sheet.

Brush with a little beaten egg
and water mixture.

9. Dips and Spreads

There was a time when "bread" automatically brought "butter" to mind, but that was then. These days, many people prefer healthy, cholesterol-free alternatives, so this chapter includes some enticing choices for you to offer with your homemade bread.

The simplest, of course, is good-quality extra-virgin olive oil for dipping. Ubiquitous in restaurants, it's just as good at home. And there are many other options. A dish of mellow Roasted Garlic, for example, to squeeze directly from the cloves onto bread is a sure winner.

For entertaining, you will find that the dips in this chapter make wonderful party food. For your next cocktail event try serving Tzatziki or Hummus with Pita (page 112), or Baba Ghanoush with your homemade Lavash (page 114), Pideh (page 116), or Matzoh (page 117).

For a brunch featuring your handmade Bagels (pages 126 and 128), you will want to serve classic spreads like Cream Cheese and Chives and Cream Cheese and Smoked Salmon. And last, but always lovely, is the elegant tea party with, of course, Scones (page 110) laden with jam and (not exactly cholesterol-free) Clotted Cream.

TZATZIKI

This popular Greek yogurt dip is most often served with pita, but is delicious with any bread.

YIELD: ABOUT 2 CUPS

2 cups plain yogurt

1 tablespoon olive oil

1 tablespoon lemon juice

1 medium cucumber, peeled, seeds removed, and finely chopped

1 tablespoon minced garlic

1–2 tablespoons finely chopped fresh dill

Salt and pepper to taste

1. Place all the ingredients in medium bowl and mix with a whisk or fork until well blended.

2. Refrigerate until well chilled.

ROASTED GARLIC

A special treat for garlic lovers who dislike the lingering taste and aroma of raw garlic.

YIELD: 6 HEADS

6 heads garlic

3 tablespoons olive oil

Salt and pepper to taste

1. Preheat the oven to 325°F.

2. With a sharp knife, cut off the top quarter of each garlic head so the cloves are exposed and peel off the loose papery skin. Place the heads cut side up in a small baking dish, drizzle with olive oil, then sprinkle with salt and pepper.

3. Cover the dish with foil. Roast for 1 hour, then remove the foil and roast for another 10 to 15 minutes, or until the cloves are soft and light brown. Remove from oven and let cool.

4. Release the softened cloves by gently squeezing them (right onto the bread). Spread with a butter knife.

HUMMUS

Although this Middle-Eastern chick-pea spread is traditionally served with pita,
it goes well with just about any type of bread or cracker.

1. Place the chick peas, tahini, garlic, lemon juice, oil, salt, and pepper into a food processor and blend until smooth. Use a little of the reserved chick-pea liquid as needed to achieve the desired consistency.

2. Transfer to a small serving bowl, sprinkle with parsley, and serve.

YIELD: ABOUT 2 CUPS

2 cups cooked chick peas (or 20-ounce can), drained, with liquid reserved

$\frac{1}{2}$ cup tahini

1 clove garlic, or to taste

Juice of 2 lemons (about $\frac{1}{4}$ cup)

2 tablespoons olive oil

$\frac{1}{2}$ teaspoon salt, or to taste

$\frac{1}{4}$ teaspoon freshly ground pepper, or to taste

Chopped parsley for garnish

CLOTTED CREAM

This treat is cream that has had most of its water removed so it is extra rich.
It isn't diet food, but it's good.

1. Fit a cone-shaped coffee filter into a funnel and stand it up in a jar or glass. Pour the heavy cream into the filter, cover, and refrigerate for five or six hours, or until the whey separates and runs into the jar.

2. Scoop the clotted cream from the filter, place in a bowl, and serve.

YIELD: ABOUT 1 $\frac{1}{2}$ CUPS

2 cups heavy cream

BABA GHANOUSH

You can make this wonderful bread accompaniment by hand, as directed in this recipe,
or simply place all of the ingredients in a food processor and pulse to a thick purée.

YIELD: ABOUT 2 CUPS

1 medium eggplant, pricked all
   over with a fork

1 large garlic clove, pressed or
   finely minced, and squashed
   with the side of a knife

Juice of 1 lemon (2–3 tablespoons)

2-inch pita wedge or half slice
   bread, crumbled

¼ cup chopped parsley

Salt to taste

Pepper to taste

Chopped parsley for garnish

1. Microwave the eggplant about 10 minutes, or until it is soft. Let cool until you can handle it comfortably.

2. Scoop the flesh into a bowl, add the garlic, and mash with a potato masher. Add the bread and lemon juice, and continue to mash and stir the mixture until well blended.

3. Stir in the parsley, salt, and pepper. Garnish with more parsley and serve.

Olive Oil Dips

For those who prefer an alternative to butter on their bread, there is nothing better than good-quality extra-virgin olive oil for dipping. Try experimenting with different kinds—Italian, French, Spanish, and Greek olive oils have their own distinctive character and all are readily available. Try different brands, too, until you find the one you like best. For variety, you can add any number of flavorful ingredients to the oil, such as chopped fresh rosemary, sage, or basil; Greek, French, or Italian olives; grated Parmigiano cheese with a grind or two of fresh black pepper; a sprinkle of crushed red pepper; or a dash of pesto. The sky is pretty much the limit!

CLASSIC BAGEL SPREADS

You can make these wonderful bread accompaniments by hand, as directed in this recipe, or simply place all of the ingredients in a food processor and pulse to a thick purée.

CREAM CHEESE & CHIVES

YIELD: ABOUT 1 CUP

1. Add the chives to the cream cheese and blend together with a fork.

2. Use right away or cover and refrigerate up to five days.

8-ounce container whipped cream cheese

$\frac{1}{4}$ cup finely minced chives

CREAM CHEESE & SMOKED SALMON (LOX)

YIELD: ABOUT 1 CUP

1. Add the smoked salmon to the cream cheese and blend together with a fork.

2. Use right away or cover and refrigerate up to five days.

8-ounce container whipped cream cheese

4 ounces smoked salmon, minced

TIP Alternatively, and even easier than making this spread, just serve a bowl of cream cheese and a platter of smoked salmon with lemon wedges. Nova Scotia smoked salmon is less salty than regular and is often preferred. It is commonly served with Greek olives and sliced tomatoes.

METRIC CONVERSION TABLES

Common Liquid Conversions

Measurement	=	Milliliters
¼ teaspoon	=	1.25 milliliters
½ teaspoon	=	2.50 milliliters
¾ teaspoon	=	3.75 milliliters
1 teaspoon	=	5.00 milliliters
1 ¼ teaspoons	=	6.25 milliliters
1 ½ teaspoons	=	7.50 milliliters
1 ¾ teaspoons	=	8.75 milliliters
2 teaspoons	=	10.0 milliliters
1 tablespoon	=	15.0 milliliters
2 tablespoons	=	30.0 milliliters

Measurement	=	Liters
¼ cup	=	0.06 liters
½ cup	=	0.12 liters
¾ cup	=	0.18 liters
1 cup	=	0.24 liters
1 ¼ cups	=	0.30 liters
1 ½ cups	=	0.36 liters
2 cups	=	0.48 liters
2 ½ cups	=	0.60 liters
3 cups	=	0.72 liters
3 ½ cups	=	0.84 liters
4 cups	=	0.96 liters
4 ½ cups	=	1.08 liters
5 cups	=	1.20 liters
5 ½ cups	=	1.32 liters

Converting Fahrenheit to Celsius

Fahrenheit	=	Celsius
200–205	=	95
220–225	=	105
245–250	=	120
275	=	135
300–305	=	150
325–330	=	165
345–350	=	175
370–375	=	190
400–405	=	205
425–430	=	220
445–450	=	230
470–475	=	245
500	=	260

Conversion Formulas

LIQUID When You Know	Multiply By	To Determine
teaspoons	5.0	milliliters
tablespoons	15.0	milliliters
fluid ounces	30.0	milliliters
cups	0.24	liters
pints	0.47	liters
quarts	0.95	liters

WEIGHT When You Know	Multiply By	To Determine
ounces	28.0	grams
pounds	0.45	kilograms

Index

THE WHOLE HERB
For Cooking, Crafts, Gardening, Health, and Other Joys of Life
Barbara Pleasant

Herbs are nature's pure and precious gifts. They provide sustenance for both our bodies and our souls. They have been our medicine and our food. Their fragrance and beauty have warmed our hearts and delighted our senses.

The Whole Herb is a complete, practical, and easy-to-follow guide to the many uses of these wonderful treasures of the earth. It presents their fascinating history, as well as their many uses, including herbs and health, herbs and cooking, herbs around the house, and herbs in the garden. A comprehensive A-to-Z reference profiles over fifty commonly used and affordable herb varieties. Each entry provides specific information on the herb's background, benefits, and uses, along with helpful buying guides, growing instructions, preservation methods, and safety information.

Whether you want to use herbs to create better health, better meals, unforgettable fragrances, impressive crafts, or a beautiful garden, *The Whole Herb* is here to help.

$14.95 US / $22.50 CAN • 252 pages • 7.5 x 7.5-inch paperback • 2-Color • ISBN 0-7570-0080-0

GOING WILD IN THE KITCHEN
The Fresh & Sassy Tastes of Vegetarian Cooking
Leslie Cerier

Going Wild in the Kitchen is the first comprehensive global vegetarian cookbook to go beyond the standard organic beans, grains, and vegetables. In addition to providing helpful cooking tips and techniques, the book contains over 200 kitchen-tested recipes for healthful, taste-tempting dishes—creative masterpieces that contain such unique ingredients as edible flowers; sea vegetables; wild mushrooms, berries, and herbs; and goat and sheep cheeses. It encourages the creative side of novice and seasoned cooks alike, prompting them to follow their instincts and "go wild" in the kitchen by adding, changing, or substituting ingredients in existing recipes. To help, a wealth of suggestions is found throughout. Beautiful color photographs and a helpful resource list for finding organic foods complete this user-friendly cookbook.

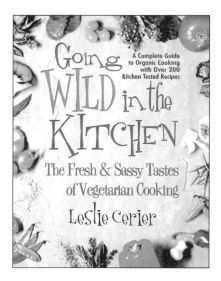

Going Wild in the Kitchen is both a unique cookbook and a recipe for inspiration. So let yourself go! Excite your palate with this treasure-trove of unique, healthy, and taste-tempting recipe creations.

$16.95 US / $25.50 CAN • 240 pages • 7.5 x 9-inch paperback • 2-Color • ISBN 0-7570-0091-6

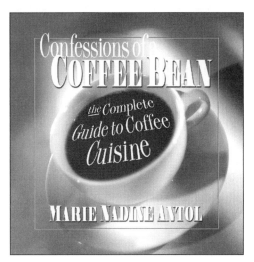

CONFESSIONS OF A COFFEE BEAN
The Complete Guide to Coffee Cuisine
Marie Nadine Antol

Yes, I have a few things to confess. But before I start, I just want you to know that I couldn't help it. It just happened. Everywhere I went, they wanted me. Whether it was my full body or my distinctive aroma, I can't tell you. All I know is that no matter where you go in this crazy mixed-up world, they all want coffee. Now, I have a few things to share—I think it's time to spill the beans.

Our love affair with coffee continues to blossom. From coast to coast, the growing number of coffee bars serves as a shining testament to this glorious romance. And now we have a wonderful new book that explores all things coffee. *Confessions of a Coffee Bean* is a complete guide to understanding and appreciating this object of our affection. It provides a fascinating history of the bean and its lore. It looks at the uniqueness of coffee houses found around the world—from Turkey to Germany to England. It details the various types of coffee available, as well as the best way to brew each to its own distinct perfection. It then concludes with over sixty enticing recipes that celebrate the very taste that is coffee.

$13.95 US / $20.95 CAN • 204 pages • 7.5 x 7.5-inch quality paperback • 2-Color • ISBN 0-7570-0020-7

FOR THE LOVE OF GARLIC
The Complete Guide to Garlic Cuisine
Victoria Renoux

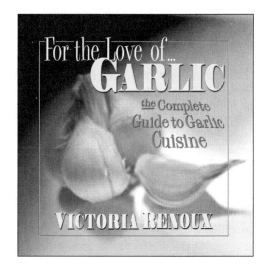

For the Love of Garlic is a celebration of an astonishingly versatile food. It explores garlic's past and present, and provides a wide variety of delicious kitchen-tested garlic recipes designed to tempt not only garlic aficionados, but all lovers of great cuisine.

Part One begins by looking at the history, lore, and many uses of this culinary treasure. It examines how garlic's active compounds have been proven to heal illness and maintain radiant health. Also included is a section on growing and buying this gourmet marvel. Part Two indulges in the tastes and pleasures of garlic. The author first discusses cooking techniques and special utensils that can enhance the use of this ingredient. She then offers eighty-five tempting dishes that will allow you to indulge all your garlic fantasies.

Whether given as a gift or used as a personal reference, this beautifully designed and illustrated work will prove itself to be a useful and informative guide time and time again.

$13.95 US / $20.95 CAN • 204 pages • 7.5 x 7.5-inch quality paperback • 2-Color • ISBN 0-7570-0087-8

TALES OF A TEA LEAF
The Complete Guide to Tea Cuisine
Jill Yates

For devoted tea drinkers everywhere, *Tales of a Tea Leaf*—a complete guide to the intricacies of tea lore, tea brewing, and tea cuisine—is here. The book begins with an exploration of the legends and lore of tea, including its mysterious age-old relationship with rebels and smugglers. It presents the many tea types and brewing methods, as well as the miraculous health benefits of the tea leaf. What follows next is a collection of delicious tea beverages, from refreshing iced drinks to warm, spicy brews, as well as other wonderful creations, such as Apricot Tea Bread and Pumpkin Chai Pie. One thing is certain—you don't need to be a tea lover to enjoy *Tales of a Tea Leaf.*

$13.95 US / $20.95 CAN • 204 pages • 7.5 x 7.5-inch quality paperback • 2-Color • ISBN 0-7570-0099-1

THE SOPHISTICATED OLIVE
The Complete Guide to Olive Cuisine
Marie Nadine Antol

Simple. Elegant. Refined. It has truly evolved into a most sophisticated food. It is the olive. With a history as old as the Bible, the humble olive has matured into a culinary treasure. Enter any fine restaurant and there you will find the sumptuous flavor of olives in cocktails, appetizers, salads, entrées, and so much more. Now, food writer Marie Nadine Antol has created an informative guide to this glorious fruit's many healthful benefits, surprising uses, and spectacular tastes.

Part One of the book begins by exploring the rich and fascinating history and lore of the olive—from its endearing Greek and Roman legends to its many biblical citations to its place in the New World. It then looks at the olive plant and its range of remarkable properties, covering its uses as a beauty enhancer and a health provider. The book goes on to describe the many varieties of olives that are found around the world, examining their oils, flavors, and interesting characteristics. Part One concludes by providing you with everything you need to know to grow your own olive tree—just like Thomas Jefferson.

Part Two offers over one hundred kitchen-tested recipes designed to put a smile on the face of any olive lover. It first explains the many ways olives can be cured at home. It then covers a host of salads, dressings, tapenades and spreads, soups, side dishes, entrées, breads, cakes, and, of course, beverages to wind down with. So whether you are an olive aficionado or just a casual olive eater, we know you'll be pleased to discover the many new faces of *The Sophisticated Olive.*

$13.95 US / $20.95 CAN • 204 pages • 7.5 x 7.5-inch quality paperback • 2-Color • ISBN 0-7570-0024-X

KITCHEN QUICKIES
Great, Satisfying Meals in Minutes
Marie Caratozzolo and Joanne Abrams

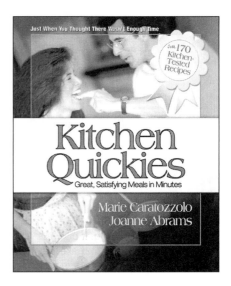

Ever feel that there aren't enough hours in the day to enjoy life's pleasures—simple or otherwise? Whether you're dealing with problems on the job, chasing after kids on the home front, or simply running from errand to errand, the evening probably finds you longing for a great meal, but with neither the time nor the desire to prepare one.

Kitchen Quickies offers a solution. Virtually all of its over 170 kitchen-tested recipes—yes, really kitchen tested—call for a maximum of only five main ingredients other than kitchen staples, and each dish takes just minutes to prepare! Imagine being able to whip up dishes like Southwestern Tortilla Pizzas, Super Salmon Burgers, and Tuscan-Style Fusilli—in no time flat! As a bonus, these delicious dishes are actually good for you—low in fat and high in nutrients!

So the next time you think that there's simply no time to cook a great meal, pick up *Kitchen Quickies.* Who knows? You may even have time for a few "quickies" of your own.

$14.95 US / $22.50 CAN • 240 pages • 7.5 x 9-inch quality paperback • Full-color photos • ISBN 0-7570-0085-1

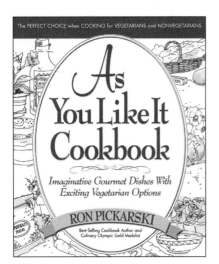

AS YOU LIKE IT COOKBOOK
Imaginative Gourmet Dishes with Exciting Vegetarian Options
Ron Pickarski

When it comes to food, we certainly like to have it our way. However, catering to individual tastes can pose quite a challenge for the cook. The *As You Like It Cookbook* is designed to help you meet the challenge of cooking for both vegetarians and nonvegetarians alike. It offers over 170 great-tasting dishes that cater to a broad range of tastes. Many of the easy-to-follow recipes are vegetarian—and offer ingredient alternatives for meat eaters. Conversely, recipes that include meat, poultry, or fish offer nonmeat ingredient options. Furthermore, if the recipe includes eggs or dairy products, a vegan alternative is provided. This book has it all—delicious breakfast favorites, satisfying soups and sandwiches, mouth-watering entrées, and delectable desserts.

With one or two simple ingredient substitutions, the *As You Like It Cookbook* will show you how easy it is to transform satisfying meat dishes into delectable meatless fare, and vegetarian dishes into meat-lover's choices.

$16.95 US / $25.50 CAN • 216 pages • 7.5 x 9-inch quality paperback • Full-color photos • ISBN 0-7570-0013-4

MRS. CUBBISON'S BEST STUFFING COOKBOOK

Sensational Stuffings for Poultry, Meats, Fish, Side Dishes, and More

Edited by Leo Pearlstein and Lisa Messinger

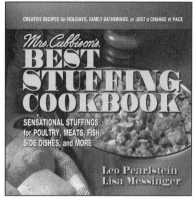

When you think of stuffing, you probably picture Thanksgiving, turkey, and traditional dinner fare. But now that people all over the country are enjoying exciting new flavors, from fusion cooking to ethnic cuisine, maybe it's time to add a little pizzazz to your stuffing—and to your everyday meals, as well! Designed to take stuffing to new culinary heights, here is a superb collection of creative recipes from America's number-one stuffing expert, Mrs. Sophie Cubbison.

Mrs. Cubbison's Best Stuffing Cookbook is a complete guide to the art of making delicious stuffing. It begins with the basics of preparing stuffing from convenient mixes, and then offers more than one hundred easy-to-make kitchen-tested recipes not just for side-dish stuffings, but also for delectable entrées ranging from Blackened Turkey Breast With Jambalaya Stuffing to Poached Salmon With Dill Stuffing. Mrs. Cubbison even guides you in turning stuffing into mouth-watering muffins, appetizers, and desserts!

For over forty years, pioneering chef Mrs. Cubbison reinvented the way we cook with stuffing. Today, her work, her creativity, and her namesake company live on to reflect our ever-evolving tastes. With *Mrs. Cubbison's Best Stuffing Cookbook* in hand, you can add a touch of creativity not only to your holiday celebrations, but to every meal that you and your family enjoy.

$14.95 US / $22.50 CAN • 156 Pages • 7.5 x 7.5-inch quality paperback • ISBN 0-7570-0260-9

THE SOURDOUGH BREAD BOWL COOKBOOK

For Parties, Holiday Celebrations, Family Gatherings, and Everyday Meals

John Vrattos and Lisa Messinger

For decades, visitors to San Francisco's famed Fisherman's Wharf have enjoyed piping hot clam chowder served in a crusty sourdough bread bowl. As the popularity of this culinary treat grew, so did the many creative uses of bread bowls—from centerpieces filled with luscious dips to edible vessels for salads, entrées, and more. Gourmet cook John Vrattos and best-selling food writer Lisa Messinger have created a cookbook to show you how. After presenting easy-to-follow instructions for carving out a bread bowl, they offer over 100 sumptuous kitchen-tested recipes, ranging from traditional dishes such as Fisherman's Wharf-Style Clam Chowder to innovative creations like Teriyaki Chicken Bowl and Popcorn Shrimp Gumbo. Throughout the book, you'll also find outstanding bread bowl recipes developed by a number of top restaurant chefs.

Whether you're hosting a Super Bowl party, preparing a meal for the family, or simply cooking an intimate dinner for two, make your event a little more special with a selection from *The Sourdough Bread Bowl Cookbook.*

$14.95 US / $22.50 CAN • 156 Pages • 7.5 x 7.5-inch quality paperback • ISBN 0-7570-0149-1

THE MASON JAR COOKBOOK SERIES
Lonnette Parks

The popularity of Mason jar mixes is taking the country by storm! These beautifully decorated jars are filled with attractive layers of ingredients for making a variety of scrumptious kitchen creations. Topped with an eye-catching square of fabric that is tied on with decorative twine or ribbon, these jars are a pleasure to give and a joy to receive.

If you've ever wanted to create beautiful Mason gift jars in your own home, or try your hand at making the recipes yourself, here's the good news: You don't have to be a craft expert to assemble the containers, nor do you have to be a culinary school graduate to prepare the recipes in your own kitchen. Best-selling writer Lonnette Parks shows you just how easy it is. In her first book, *The Mason Jar Cookie Cookbook*, Lonnette shares fifty of her favorite cookie recipes. In her second book, *The Mason Jar Soup-to-Nuts Cookbook*, she presents fifty fantastic recipes for soups, muffins, breads, beverages, cakes, and more. Now, in her latest title, *The Mason Jar Dessert Cookbook*, Lonnette offers fifty delectable new dessert recipes guaranteed to put a smile on your face. Just like the other books in the series, this one is designed for both the cook and the crafter. Each recipe includes easy-to-follow directions for creating the jarred mix. You'll learn what size jar to use and how to make neat ingredient layers. Then Lonnette will show you how to add those finishing touches that turn the jar into a beautiful gift.

Whether you want to prepare the Mason jar recipes yourself or create impressive gift jars for family and friends, The Mason Jar Cookbook Series is all you need. Enjoy the experience!

THE MASON JAR COOKIE COOKBOOK

$12.95 US / $21.00 CAN • 144 pages • 7.5 x 7.5-inch quality paperback
2-Color • ISBN 0-7570-0046-0

THE MASON JAR SOUP-TO-NUTS COOKBOOK

$12.95 US / $21.00 CAN • 144 pages • 7.5 x 7.5-inch quality paperback
2-Color • ISBN 0-7570-0129-7

THE MASON JAR DESSERT COOKBOOK

$12.95 US / $21.00 CAN • 144 pages • 7.5 x 7.5-inch quality paperback
2-Color • ISBN 0-7570-0295-1

For more information about our books, visit our website at www.squareonepublishers.com